MW00816931

Memorize
—what—
Matters

12 Proven Strategies to Memorize the Bible

JOSH SUMMERS

Jesus answered, "It is written: 'Man shall not live on bread alone, but on every word that comes from the mouth of God.'"

Matthew 4:4, Deuteronomy 8:3

Memorize What Matters
© 2024 by Josh Summers

ISBN 978-1-7321204-8-8 (hard cover)
ISBN 978-1-7321204-7-1 (soft cover)
ISBN 978-1-7321204-6-4 (audio)
ISBN 978-1-7321204-5-7 (ebook)

All Scripture quotations, unless otherwise indicated, are taken from the Holy Bible, New International Version®, NIV®. Copyright ©1973, 1978, 1984, 2011 by Biblica, Inc.™ Used by permission of Zondervan. All rights reserved worldwide. www.zondervan.com "NIV" and "New International Version" are trademarks registered in the United States Patent and Trademark Office by Biblica, Inc.™

Scripture quotations marked (ESV) are from the ESV® Bible (The Holy Bible, English Standard Version®), © 2001 by Crossway, a publishing ministry of Good News Publishers. Used by permission. All rights reserved.

John Outline images from Chapter 2 Copyright © 2024 by Larry Dinkins. www.oralstoryteller.org Used by permission.

All rights reserved. No portion of this book may be reproduced in any form without written permission from the publisher or author, except as permitted by U.S. copyright laws.

Cover Design: Sarah Immanuel
Interior Art: Emily Mills
Editor: Vicki Newby

First printing September 2024

Praise for Memorize What Matters:

Memorize What Matters is one of the most compelling and helpful books about Scripture memory I've ever read. Whether you're brand new to Scripture memory or you've been memorizing for years, this book is an invaluable resource filled with the encouragement and practical tools you need to get God's Word where it belongs: in your heart.

Dakota Lynch
Executive Director, Scripture Memory Fellowship

This book is a brilliant resource for every believer in Christ! If you've ever been intimidated by memorizing Scripture, Josh's creative and thoughtful approach will make it practical and accessible. He'll give you the tools and confidence you need to tuck God's Word into your heart, and you will be wiser and richer because of it.

Jennifer Rothschild
Best-selling author, speaker and podcast host

I can't think of a discipline that promises greater reward than committing God's Word to memory. *Memorize What Matters* provides motivation, strategies, and practical tools to either begin or renew a lifelong habit of internalizing Scripture. Josh encourages Christians to cultivate a growing appetite for the nourishment that really matters!

Steve Richardson
President, Pioneers International

Josh is a man who has spent years studying how to memorize scripture. He has interviewed dozens of practitioners in the art and has become an expert himself. This book will disclose twelve of his most effective practical methods for committing God's perfect word to your mind and heart. His book is extremely readable, engaging, creative, and actionable. I look forward to recommending it to others who want to begin this journey but don't know how.

Dr. Andy Davis
Pastor & Author, How to Memorize Scripture for Life

What a great resource! Josh's book includes the WHY and lots of HOW options. It will stretch your perception of Scripture memory and make your goals more achievable. I can't wait to share it with my Scripture memory group!

Janet Pope
Author, His Word in My Heart

This book is another excellent example of how Josh is inspiring the Church to hide God's Word in their heart.

Prof. Tom Meyer
The Bible Memory Man

Josh has talked with more experts in Bible memorization than anyone I know and, in the course of applying their insights, become an expert himself. I cannot recommend this short book more highly. In these pages you will find a treasure trove of tried-and-true methods for Bible memory. If you take them seriously, these tools will equip you to not merely eek by but to thrive while memorizing the Bible.

Joshua Frost
Missionary, Bible translator, and Researcher

Contents

Prologue   3

Introduction   9

Unexpected Benefits   15

What's Your P.O.I.N.T.?   29

The Understanding Pyramid   37

1. First-Letter Method   49

2. Visual Outline Method   55

3. Speak It Out Loud   69

4. Memorize Like an Actor   77

5. Write Them on the Doorframes   87

6. Record and Listen   95

7. Sing the Bible   103

8. Print the Page and Mark It Up   111

9. Puzzle Patterns   121

10. Mind Palace   133

11. Spaced Repetition   147

12. Celebrate Your Wins   157

Epilogue   167

Have I not commanded you? Be strong and courageous. Do not be afraid; do not be discouraged, for the Lord your God will be with you wherever you go.

Joshua 1:9

Prologue
Detained

"Put your backpack on the table. Hand over your camera, your phone, and anything else in your pockets." A short pause and then, "*NOW!*" A Chinese police officer barked orders at me with force. He stared at me without blinking while I complied.

He led me down the staircase to the dark basement of the police station.

We passed by a holding cell occupied by a lone man who didn't even look up as we walked by. The cell was no larger than a walk-in closet with a concrete slab just long enough for one person to lie down. I saw a metal toilet but nothing else. No TV. No window. No books.

Adjacent cells were empty. I was half expecting to be placed in one. I'm certain that this slow march to my destination was intentionally designed to strike fear in anyone who came through. It was working. I was scared and worried about my unknown future. Was this what I had to look forward to?

We stopped in front of a large, heavy door while the police officer fumbled with his keys. Looking up, I realized we weren't alone. Cameras had been following our entrance into this depressing place, which was ironic. A camera is what got me into this mess in the first place.

With the door finally unlocked, the officer slowly opened it and motioned for me to sit in a metal chair. The room was a concrete box with nothing on the walls except a two-way mirror and another camera in the corner. A large metal desk filled most of the room. A chair was placed on each side. The door slammed shut with authority. I heard the lock click.

I was alone.

Seconds turned into minutes which turned into hours. It's hard to describe what happened in my mind, even during the relatively short time of isolation so far, isolation I couldn't control. I started by retracing what had led me here: a local religious festival in a politically sensitive part of China. This area had been my home for years, and it was a hobby of mine to capture cultural events with my camera. This time, however, the local police decided that I had crossed some invisible line, perhaps believing that I was working for some government or foreign news publication. They threw me into a van and drove me to this police station without even giving me time to call my wife.

Oh, my goodness! My wife! My boys!

How would they know where I was? They wouldn't know I was missing until later that evening when I didn't come home. Would they be taken as well?

Panic started to rise from my stomach into my throat, and I desperately grasped for anything to calm me down. "God, what's happening here?" I prayed. I didn't have my Bible with me, and my electronic devices had been confiscated, so I was forced to draw from the well of whatever I had stored in my memory.

I began to take inventory of what I could remember, not knowing how many more hours, days, or even weeks this isolation would continue.

Sadly, despite having grown up in a Christian household and attending Sunday school every week, I could barely come up with 20 Bible verses to calm my spirit.

My mind wandered to the man in the cell just outside the locked door, wondering if I would soon be joining him. What if these 20 verses were all I would have of my faith to sustain me during this time? That most certainly wouldn't be enough. Why hadn't I been more intentional about internalizing God's Word?

This sobering moment in the basement of a Chinese police station was the exact moment I decided to make memorizing the Bible a priority.

Hear More of the Story

 More of this story will be shared throughout the book, but you can listen to a 2-part podcast episode where I dive deeper into the details of this interrogation. Scan the QR code here or visit:

MemorizeWhatMatters.com/interrogated

Let us not become weary in doing good, for at the proper time we will reap a harvest if we do not give up.

Galatians 5:9

Introduction
Build Your Boat

It may be unlikely that you'll ever be detained by a foreign government and stripped of your Bible. Lord willing, we won't live to see the day when Bibles are removed from bookshelves or banned altogether.

Each of us, however, will inevitably experience seasons of life where our access to the Bible is either limited or completely cut off. Consider one of these more relatable scenarios:

— That season as a new parent when you can't get more than 5 minutes of quiet amid the constant feedings, diapers, and errands. While pacing the nursery with a baby in hand for the third sleepless night in a row, you realize you haven't cracked your Bible open in a week...or a month.

— That season in your working career when you have to put in another 14-hour workday to hit the next deadline. The stress continues to mount, and the only free moment you might have is a 30-minute commute when it's impossible to pull out a Bible to read.

— That season of doctor visits after an unexpected accident or illness. The hours undergoing treatment or surgery are almost as lonely as the time spent recovering in bed. You barely have the energy to get up, go to church, or get any kind of spiritual nourishment.

— That season of spiritual attack when the voices in your head continually spew lies that go unchallenged by the truths of the Bible. It feels impossible to pull out your Bible to find the right verse to defend yourself all the time.

— That moment during a conversation with a friend when you sense the opportunity to share your faith or pray a psalm over them, but you either don't have your Bible or if you did, you wouldn't know exactly where to turn.

We can plan for some of these scenarios, but in most cases, real life takes us completely by surprise.

That's what happened to my friend Jill Donovan. A few years ago, she felt this internal nudge to start memorizing the Bible, a spiritual practice she knew was valuable but hadn't set aside time to develop. She started slowly but remained disciplined over time, not realizing that less than a year later, the unthinkable would turn her world upside down.

She got the call from her doctor that her scans had come back positive for cancer. Like most cancer patients, she was completely blindsided. Her life suddenly became a flurry of doctor visits and chemotherapy treatments. The verses she had memorized were no longer just a fun brain exercise, they became a lifeline for her during a time when she often couldn't pull out her Bible.

Jill summarized her experience on the Memorize What Matters podcast in a way that deeply resonated with me: "*When God tells you to build a boat, you better do it because you never know when the rains will come.*"[1]

---

1. Watch the full interview with Jill here: MemorizeWhatMatters.com/Jill

Investing your time toward memorizing God's Word is not wasted effort, even if you don't see storm clouds on the horizon. It will never return empty. Meditating and internalizing the Bible prepares us for the unexpected rain. It prepares us for those divine conversations, those spiritual battles, or those moments when our faith is being shaken.

Most importantly, the double-edged sword of the Word prepares our hearts to be transformed by the power of the gospel.

Consider this your call to start building a boat. Thankfully, you'll find that rain isn't the only thing you have to look forward to. There are plenty of wonderful and unexpected benefits to Bible memory as well.

Do you not know that in a race all the runners run, but only one gets the prize? Run in such a way as to get the prize.

1 Corinthians 9:24

Unexpected Benefits

I did it! The elation of crossing the finish line almost made me forget that I had spent the past four hours torturing my body while running through the streets of Nashville. My girlfriend, who would later become my wife, met me with a hug. "I can't believe you did that," she said.

Honestly, I couldn't believe it either. For reasons I can't fully explain now, I had decided during my years at university that running a marathon would be a great goal to set for graduation. A marathon is a grueling 26.2-mile race that requires months of dedicated training and planning. You don't just show up on race day without having prepared.

And here's the thing: there's no *good time* to train for a marathon. It's always going to be hard, and it will always require time that never feels available. It's an easy goal to set but a difficult one to complete.

Knowing this, a friend and I agreed to run the race together and keep each other accountable to the training schedule it would require. Multiple times a week, we would wake up early in the morning to run miles around the city, finishing in time to eat a good breakfast and head to classes for the day.

A few months later we stood side by side with medals around our necks, a prize given to marathon runners for simply finishing—not winning—the race. Yes, we had completed our goal, but with the clarity of hindsight, we gained so many other benefits along the way.

For one, I was healthier. But more than that, I had learned how to eat better, sleep more, and push through pain. Training for a marathon gave me better mental focus during class, and it forced me to be disciplined about my time.

When it comes to Bible memorization, there are many reasons why a person might start to prioritize this spiritual discipline, whether it's the constant access to God's Word mentioned earlier, the desire to build a stronger faith foundation, or simply a love for the book.

Having a clear understanding of *your* reason why is going to help you maintain motivation over the long term when the excitement of your initial Bible memory journey starts to fade. Life begins to crowd out any available time, and it seems like progress is slow.

But similar to a marathon, consistency over time yields so many benefits that go beyond the reason why you started. In my personal experience, every year spent memorizing the Bible unlocks new blessings that I never sought or anticipated.

Here is a glimpse of some of the benefits you can expect to receive from your commitment to Bible memory.

Deeper Connection with God's Word

I've done it before. I sat down to read the Bible for 10 or 15 minutes, only to realize when I finished that I have no idea what I just read. My eyes scanned the words, but my mind never processed the concepts. You've experienced that too?

To be fair, it's possible to do the same thing when memorizing a verse or passage, but I've found it to be much less likely. While memorizing and reviewing a verse word for word, I'm forced to think critically about why a particular word was used, why the author phrased a statement the way he did, or even why it's in the present tense or the past tense.

For example, when memorizing Psalm 46, which is my favorite of all the psalms, the first seven verses are written in the present tense: "God *is* our refuge," "Nations *are* in uproar," "The Lord Almighty *is* with us." I noticed a slight change in verse 8. I would have expected that verse to continue with the present continuous tense (hey, I know my grammar!), reading "Come and see *what the Lord is doing.*"

Instead, the verse moves into a different tense. "Come and see what the Lord *has done.*"

That's a subtle difference that I've skipped hundreds of times when I've read that passage before, but it's impossible to ignore when I'm memorizing it. I believe a theological truth is hidden in that simple change of verb tense. An explanation about the theology of it is beyond the scope of this book, but this deeper connection with God's Word is something I've run across multiple times while memorizing.

Building Biblical Connections

God has wired your brain to seek connections. Your brain is constantly looking for what is familiar, whether it's the face of a person you know, a smell that triggers a childhood memory, or a movie quote that fits the context of a conversation.

Your mind keeps a database of these important memories or ideas; some you can retrieve easily, and others hidden so deep that you only remember when the magnetic force of a connection is so strong that it pulls it to the surface of your conscious awareness.

Memorizing the Bible is one of the best ways to fill this database with biblical truths that will come to mind even at the most random of moments. There's a physiological explanation for how this happens, but a spiritual component to this is found in John 14:26. "But the Advocate, the Holy Spirit, whom the Father will send in my name, will teach you all things and will remind you of everything I have said to you."

The key word here is *remind*. The Spirit can only remind us of something that we have stored in our memory, and I believe that can even be done with verses we think we've forgotten.

One of the greatest joys I experience when studying the Bible these days are the moments of surprise when I read a passage and find myself thinking, *that sounds exactly like something Paul said in his second letter to Timothy* or *that reminds me of something Jesus said in the Gospel of John.*

The more of God's Word that I memorize, the more this happens, which deepens my understanding and love for the Bible even further.

Owning a Passage

There's something special about listening to a sermon or being in a conversation when the speaker mentions a passage of Scripture that I previously memorized. Because my brain craves connection, the moment I hear the passage, I get a rush of dopamine as my mind sends an instant message to my consciousness. *Hey! I've memorized this before. This is* my *passage.*

That great feeling can happen to you too. It comes from the sense that I have become the owner of that part of the Bible because I've memorized it.

I own the book of Philippians. It's been in my memory for years now and every time someone quotes a verse from it, a smile crosses my face. *That's my book,* I think to myself. Having recited this epistle hundreds of times now, it seems like Paul is speaking directly to me. I feel his emotions, and I have a grasp of the context that passage fits into.

Every time this happens, I walk away with a holy greediness to own more.

Hearing from God

I've struggled to hear from God. I know I'm not alone in this. It feels unfair when I read stories of Moses encountering God in a burning bush or Paul hearing an audible voice from heaven. I can point to moments in my life when I have begged God for an answer only to be met with what felt like silence.

While I believe that God can communicate with people in a multitude of creative ways, I also believe that people underestimate the power we have in the gift of the written Word of God. He inspired the authors of 66 biblical books to write down *his words* so we can carry them with us. Paul tells his disciple Timothy—

> "All Scripture is God-breathed and is useful for teaching, rebuking, correcting and training in righteousness, so that the servant of God may be

thoroughly equipped for every good work" —*2 Timothy 3:16–17*

As I continue to store away more verses in my memory, I've been shocked at the kinds of conversations I can have with God. The beauty of these Scripture-based conversations is that I can walk away confident that the conversation is what God is actually saying to me.

Me: God, I'm feeling anxious about this particular situation I'm in. You know how I desire to live out my faith, but it's been hard lately with everything that's going on.,

God: In fact, everyone who wants to live a godly life in Christ Jesus will be persecuted. (2 Timothy 3:12)

Me: Yeah, but I don't feel like this is persecution. I think I'm just overwhelmed by all the pressures of work, the personal conflicts, and other responsibilities.

God: Come to me, all you who are weary and burdened, and I will give you rest. Take my yoke upon you and learn from me, for I am gentle and humble in heart, and you will find rest for your souls. For my yoke is easy and my burden is light. (Matthew 11:28–30)

Me: I know, I know. I definitely need rest. What I wouldn't give for a vacation. But that's not going to happen, so what can I do now?

God: Be still and know that I am God. I will be exalted among the nations. I will be exalted in the earth. (Psalm 46:10)

I'm amazed to have such conversations with God. You can too.

Meditation Anytime, Anywhere

The current western Christian model for so-called *quiet times* tends to stress reading the Bible either in the morning or evening, so much so that many people consider the passages from Joshua 1 to be hyperbole. "Keep this Book of the Law always on your lips; meditate on it day and night, so that you may be careful to do everything written in it." (Joshua 1:8)

We can't *actually* be in God's Word all day, right? It's simply not practical amid work, chores, parenting, and everything else we have to do throughout the day. Or is it?

This may be true if you define meditation as opening a physical Bible and reading through the words on a page. But what happens when you have stored up the Word in your heart as it says in Psalm 119:11? "I have hidden your word in my heart that I might not sin against you."

When this is true, when you have hidden Scripture in your heart, you can meditate on it anytime, anywhere.

The act of memorizing can be tedious and time-consuming at first. The reward for this investment of time, however, is the ability to carry what you own anywhere you go. Walking the dog. Sitting in traffic. Doing the dishes. Lying restlessly in bed.

When your ability to investigate God's Word no longer depends on your access to a physical Bible or digital device, the command to meditate day and night is no longer an exaggeration. It's practical.

Learning the Language of God's Love

While this chapter could easily go on for many more pages, I'll finish with this thought: I've come to experience Bible memorization as the act of learning the language of God's love.

Children learn language by mimicking the tone and words of the people who surround them. If the parents are British, the child makes typical British vowel sounds and intonation. If the family has a large vocabulary, the child likely will also. There's a strong correlation between input—the words and phrases you hear most often—and output—the words and phrases you use when you speak.

It makes sense that a consistent input of Bible verses will result in a positive output, but I have underestimated how often that would be the case—

- In the midst of trials

- As a weapon against temptation

- As words or truth that I can pray over myself and others

- As part of daily conversations

- When asked to provide counsel or advice

Taking time to internalize God's Word makes it part of your vocabulary and a useful tool, not only an offensive weapon in spiritual warfare (Ephesians 6:17) but also a guide for communicating truth to yourself and others (John 17:17).

Beyond the Benefits

Whatever your reason why and whatever the benefits you receive from memorizing the Bible, remember that we're in a marathon, not a sprint. When Paul comes to the end of his ministry, he writes this to his protégée Timothy. "I have fought the good fight, I have finished the race, I have kept the faith" (2 Timothy 4:7).

He didn't claim to have won the race. Paul was simply faithful to finish.

Let that sink in for a moment and provide a bit of comfort. The pressure is off! You don't have to complete a goal of memorizing a book of the Bible or a certain number of verses per week. The benefits of your dedication to God's Word do not depend on any measure of successful memory or retention but on being faithful over time.

Throughout the rest of this book, I want to focus on some creative, practical techniques to memorize the Bible. We're going to learn more about how our brains function and expand our understanding of what it means to *memorize what matters.*

To start, though, I want to challenge you with an unusual question: what's your P.O.I.N.T.?

Blessed is the one
 who does not walk in step with the wicked
or stand in the way that sinners take
 or sit in the company of mockers,
but whose delight is in the law of the Lord,
 and who meditates on his law day and night.

Psalm 1:1-2

What's Your P.O.I.N.T.?

For most church-going Christians, the term *Bible memory* refers to a collection of Bible verses that you memorized as a kid, usually plucked from various Old and New Testament books. While there's nothing wrong with this image, I want to take a moment to challenge your paradigm of what constitutes *Bible memory* in the first place.

You see, there's more than one way to approach Bible memory, and I've come to see value in a balanced approach that doesn't over-emphasize one particular form of internalizing God's Word. What is this P.O.I.N.T.?

Passages
Outlines
Individual verses
Narrative stories
Topical collections

Each form is a unique tool that is useful in different situations, and I believe a balanced approach requires you to understand and incorporate multiple approaches.

Passages: Memorizing Chapters or Books

Memorizing extended passages of the Bible is my personal passion and one that I encourage others to try. I find so much value in seeing a section of Scripture as a whole and within the context of the author's overall topic or argument.

Extended memorization could take the form of a single epistle (James, Ephesians), a notable chapter (Romans 8, Psalm 119) or an important passage (Sermon on the Mount). To those who have never done it before, it may seem daunting, but as we'll uncover throughout the rest of this book, there are many techniques to make this easier.

Outlines: The 30,000-Foot View

The idea of memorizing biblical outlines is foreign to most people, but outlines can be incredibly beneficial as a part of your memorization strategy. Instead of memorizing a passage word for word, you memorize the general idea or a key verse or story from each chapter.

For example, I may not be able to quote to you the story of Lazarus in the Gospel of John (yet), but I *can* tell you that it's located in John 11. I haven't yet memorized all of 1 Peter as I write this, but I *can* tell you that the argument of Jesus as the cornerstone comes from the second chapter of this epistle.

These are examples of knowing the *outline* of a book even if you can't quote the entire passage. In many cases, it's just as valuable to be able to flip directly to a story or idea in the Bible as it is to quote it. I've seen this done in two ways.

Verse Per Chapter. My friend Paul van Allen introduced me to his method of choosing one or two verses that encapsulate the theme of a chapter and memorizing that. So instead of memorizing the entire book of James, you could choose a single verse in each chapter to represent the theme of that passage.

Image per Chapter. I've done this before with the Gospel of John, and my friend Dr. Larry Dinkins has shown that this can be accomplished with all 1,189 chapters in the Bible. Instead of a single verse, you can combine an image with an idea or story to memorize a summary of each chapter. We'll dive deeper into this concept in Chapter 5, Visual Outline Method.

Individual Verses: Tried & True Method

Most people who work on memorizing the Bible start by memorizing individual verses. Perhaps you memorized a handful of verses as a child or you're starting now with 100 verses that you think are most important to know.

When memorizing individual verses, it's common to combine both the words and the reference (exact chapter and verse number) as part of the memory work, although that's not absolutely necessary.

If you're looking for a good list of individual verses to start with, you can download a free collection of 52 foundational verses every Christian should know, one for each week of the year.

 Scan this QR code to download a free collection of 52 verses or visit:

MemorizeWhatMatters.com/52verses

Narrative Stories: Orality

Throughout most of history, both within Jewish tradition and the early church, the stories and truths of the Bible were passed down orally. In fact, most of Paul's letters in the New Testament were hand-carried and read aloud to local churches. We see that in 1 Thessalonians 5:27: "I charge you before the Lord to have this letter read to all the brothers and sisters."

Even today, some cultures are literate while others still rely on an oral tradition. In all cultures, however, one thing remains the same: everybody loves a good story.

Memorizing short stories or parables in the Bible is not only fun, it's also a very effective tool for spontaneous teaching or evangelism. "You know, that reminds me of a short story in the Bible. Can I share it with you?"

Topical: Collections of Related Verses

The last form of Scripture memory is topical collections of individual verses. You may have heard of the Romans

Road,[1] a topical collection of verses from the book of Romans that walks step by step through the message of the gospel.

You can group individual verses together on any topic ranging from comfort to praise to repentance. These verses usually aren't part of the same chapter or even the same book of the Bible, but they work together to support a biblical truth you want to internalize and have ready when needed.

What's Your P.O.I.N.T.?

Perhaps this is the first time you've even considered something other than rote memorization of random Bible verses. If so, I encourage you to think about how you would like to see Scripture impact your life.

Would you like to be able to tell stories to your kids or people you meet? Then, memorize Passages or Narrative stories. Do you value moving quickly through Scripture and getting a solid grasp of the themes of each section? You'll love the Outline approach.

---

1. Essential verses of the Romans Road are Romans 3:23, 6:23, 5:8, and 10:9-10, 13.

Do you wish to be able to pray Scripture during your personal times with God or when praying over others? You may find that the Topical approach or Individual Verse approach works best.

Throughout your Bible memorization journey, you're free to move among approaches. Sometimes I like to take a break from extended memorization of a book of the Bible and focus on memorizing an outline, for the Gospel of John, for example. At the end of the day, it's unlikely anyone will give you a medal for finishing an entire book or for completing 100 individual verses. That's not the point.

The point is to immerse yourself in God's Word, and my goal is to show you the many fun and creative ways to do this. However, even the best techniques fall short if you don't understand what you're trying to internalize. The first major concept we're going to cover is known as the Understanding Pyramid.

Give me understanding to learn your commands. May those who fear you rejoice when they see me, for I have put my hope in your word.

Psalm 119:73b–74

The Understanding Pyramid

I n December 2012, the first YouTube video hit 1 billion views. Not million. *Billion.*

It was Gangnam Style, a music video by Korean pop artist Psy (pronounced *sy*) whose crazy personality and even crazier dance moves propelled the song to become a cultural phenomenon. What makes this even more impressive is that most of the people who listened to and enjoyed this song have no idea what the song is about.

The lyrics are in Korean.

Strange as it may sound, people loved the music and the dance so much that they willingly memorized the lyrics without knowing their meaning. Sometimes this kind of memorization is unplanned, while other times it's intentional.

Many kids in the Muslim majority world are trained from an early age to memorize the Qur'an word for word. Although the Qur'an is much shorter than the Bible—78,000 words in the Qur'an compared to 780,000 in the Bible (word count varies by translations)—there's no denying that this is still an impressive feat.

An interesting part of Islam, however, is the belief that the Qur'an can only be appreciated in the original Arabic language. Memorization is only done in Arabic, whether or not the child or adult understands the language.

I know some people who memorize the original Greek or Hebrew text of the Bible despite having never studied either language. While there's certainly nothing wrong with this, there's no doubt that memorizing something one does not understand is much harder and less valuable than memorizing something the person does understand.

The beauty of God's Word, which is described in Hebrews 4:12 as being "alive and active," is that on this side of heaven, we will never be able to come to a full understanding of any one verse or passage. You can be confident that no matter how many times you've repeated or studied a verse, God can reveal himself in a fresh way that deepens your understanding of that part of Scripture.

Allow that to sink in and encourage you.

When we consider that it's easier and better to understand something before trying to memorize it and recognize that we will never fully understand Scripture in this life, where does that leave us?

We're going to call it the Understanding Pyramid.

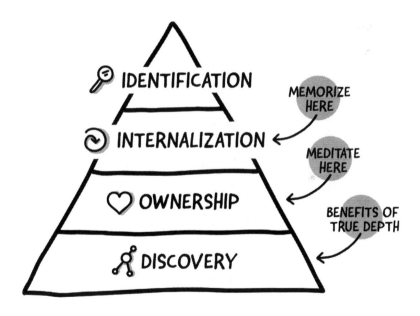

This is a concept that was born out of separate conversations with Bible teacher Keith Ferrin as well as best-selling author Jennifer Rothschild, and I consider it a foundational concept for memorizing the Bible. That's the reason why it's the first one I'm sharing with you.

The Understanding Pyramid has four levels that start from the top and expand as we go deeper: identification, internalization, ownership, and discovery.

Identification

Before I start to memorize any verse, passage, or book of the Bible, my goal is to understand it to the point of being able to identify with the passage. I have to move beyond merely reading the words before I start to memorize them.

To identify with a passage in the Bible means finding personal meaning or application. Where do I see God in these verses? How has He used this portion of the Bible to speak truth into my current situation?

Keith Ferrin modeled this for me when he shared how he spends a month reading the entire passage once every day before starting to memorize it. For example, instead of diving straight into memorizing Philippians, he spent 30 days reading through the entire letter once each day.[1]

---

1. Watch my conversation with Keith: MemorizeWhatMatters.com/Keith

This daily reading allowed him to identify key themes in the book, the general emotion of the author, and ways in which it applied to his life and circumstances. By the time he started to memorize the passage, this familiarity proved instrumental not only in the speed with which he could memorize the verses but also in his appreciation for the passage within the context of the whole story.

Consider this: before you memorize your next verse or passage, set aside a few days or weeks to read it in the context of the entire book (if it's a short one) or passage (if it's a longer book). Try to identify with the passage before you move to the next step, internalization.

Internalization

The next step in the Understanding Pyramid is to internalize the verses. I could use the word *memorize* here, but that's just one part of the equation. We memorized countless facts and figures for tests in elementary school, high school, and perhaps for university courses, but how many of those can you recall right now?

To internalize Scripture is to memorize with the intention of etching those words on your heart (Proverbs 3:3). This is accomplished by meditating on His Word day and night (Joshua 1:8).

Memorization + Meditation = Internalization

One incredible benefit of memorizing the Bible, which we covered earlier, is being able to pull out those verses anytime, anywhere. You're no longer bound by whether a physical Bible is nearby.

External factors can help the process of internalization as well. Memorizing a chapter in the book of James while your pastor or small group is doing a study on the book can be helpful. Listening to a podcast or simultaneously reading a commentary on the passage can also be beneficial as you seek to internalize it.

We're going to cover some strategies for memory review and meditation in Chapter 11, Spaced Repetition, but for now let's move onto the next level of understanding, ownership.

Ownership

Over time and with consistent meditation, God's Word will move from your head to your heart.

When this happens, it feels like you *own* that portion of the Bible.

It's yours and nobody can take it away from you! It doesn't matter if you're imprisoned for your faith, if the Bible is banned or if you simply happen to be traveling without your Bible.

The Holy Spirit can remind us of any part of Scripture that we have internalized (see John 14:26 where Jesus asserts the Holy Spirit's role of reminding the disciples of his teaching), even those parts that we think we've forgotten. However, when we *own Scripture*, those reminders seem to spring up like an overflowing well of God's wisdom.

It happens when you're in the middle of praying and suddenly a verse comes to mind that you pray out loud. It happens when you're in the middle of a conversation and a word, phrase, or idea triggers a passage that you've memorized. It happens when you're journaling, and you feel like God is speaking back to you through the words of memorized Scripture.

When God's Word is written on your heart, it's like you *own* that passage. What deeper form of understanding could there be?

Discovery

Scripture is described as a lamp in the darkness (Psalm 119:105, Proverbs 6:23) that opens our eyes to the wonderful things of God (Psalm 119:18). Even after years of memorizing extended portions of the Bible, I feel like I'm only getting momentary glimpses of this beautiful depth of understanding.

James is a book that I have had memorized for more than two decades. At this point, I've recited all five chapters at least a thousand times. I have no hesitation in telling you that I *own* the book of James.

I still learn new things when I study the book of James, but what blows me away is when I'm reading or studying a different section of Scripture, and I hear echoes of something that sounds familiar in James. For example, as I was reading through 1 Peter recently, I realized that both Peter and James seem to reference the same passage in Isaiah 40 (1 Peter 1:24, James 1:10–11, Isaiah 40:6–8).

Chances are, there's a cross-reference in your Bible next to each of those verses that confirms what I'm telling you. However, there's no comparison between the act of checking a cross-reference and the feeling of *discovering* your own cross-reference. I spent an entire, delightful afternoon digging into the context of the verses in Isaiah and the different ways that Peter and James interpreted them for their own letters. No fill-in-the-blank Bible study compares to the joy of blazing your own path through the Bible.

I'm convinced that this sense of discovery is exactly how the New Testament authors felt as they were making the connections between Jesus and the Old Testament. There were ah-ha moments of clarity when the light of God's Word opened their eyes to the truth of the gospel.

Starting the Journey

Instead of cramming a bunch of words into your head, be intentional about how you work to understand a passage of God's Word. Start by trying to identify with the verses you want to memorize and then use the internalization process to deepen your understanding of the truths and mysteries waiting to be discovered.

As you continue to meditate on what you've internalized, you will inevitably feel a sense of ownership which leads to an even deeper discovery of the beauty of Scripture.

12 Memory Strategies

So I will always remind you of these things, even though you know them and are firmly established in the truth you now have.

2 Peter 1:12

Chapter 1

First-Letter Method

An important part of building a strong memory is challenging your brain to recall a verse without having access to all the information. As benign as it seems, every time you look down at your Bible or flip the flashcard when you get stuck on a word or a verse, you're giving your brain a get-out-of-jail free card. If it doesn't have to work to produce the information on its own, it is less likely to keep it stored for long-term retrieval.

This is where a strategy like the first-letter method is so beneficial. It's a method that has been used by speakers and actors for decades to help them quickly memorize lines. It's something you can start using today to memorize verses.

Thankfully, it's also incredibly simple. Let's take a well-known verse like Romans 6:23 as an example. "For the wages of sin is death, but the gift of God is eternal life in Christ Jesus our Lord."

The first-letter method shortens everything by only writing out the first letter of each word along with any capitalization and punctuation. It would look like this:

F t w o s i d, b t g o G i e l i C J o L.

Easy, right? Despite it being so easy, though, the benefits of using this method are incredible.

- **Brain Exercise.** Your brain still has to work. The power of this method is that you can memorize and review your Bible verses without giving your brain access to *all* the information. There's still work to be done to connect the first letter with the rest of the word, and this extra step in the process is one way to help move a verse from short-term memory to long-term.

- **Less Space, Less Time.** It's significantly faster to write out the first letter of each word in a verse and it takes up less space. I know some people who find value in writing out every word of a verse or passage, but this serves as a good method for memorizing and not necessarily for reviewing.

- **Writing by Hand.** You get value from writing the first letter of the words in each verse by hand on a flashcard or in a notebook. Moving your hand and focusing on copying each letter is part of the memorization process. For those who are memorizing extended passages of Scripture, you can take this a step further by using a grid to distinguish between individual verses. In the example below, the grid is divided into five columns with the fifth column shaded in blue.

- **Recognizing or Creating Patterns.** There are many times that writing out the first letters of every word in a verse allows you to see a pattern emerge that you wouldn't have seen otherwise. We'll explore this idea more in Chapter 9, Puzzle Patterns. Additionally, you can create patterns through a grid system that breaks up each verse into its own box on a page, as seen in the following example.

Romans 1:1-15 (NIV)

1.	2.	3.	4.	5.
PasoCJ ctbaaa SaftgoG	tghpb thp iths	rhS wathel wadoJCol	awttSoh wa+SoGip bhrfta JCoL	thwrgaa tcatgtto tcfffhns
6.	7.	8.	9.	10.
ayaaatg wactb +JC	taiR walbG actbhhp: gaptyfGoF aft LJC	Fitmg +JCfaoy byfibr aotw	Gwisims iptgohS imwhciry	impaat aiptnal bawtw mbofmtcty
11.	12.	13.	14.	15.
iltsysti mityssg tm	tityaimb meboof	ldnwy	laobtgang wat5	tiwlase tptgaty

As odd as this may seem, using this kind of grid to memorize longer passages will naturally give your mind a way to break up the section you're memorizing into groups of five verses. As you review—and without any extra work on your part—the shade of blue will remain associated with the verses in that grid box, giving you a helpful marker to jump through every five verses in a passage.

In other words, as you recite a passage, when you reach a verse that was written in the blue grid box, your brain will automatically associate that blue shade with the verse and give you a clue that it is the fifth, 10th, or 15th verse in the chapter.

Take the Next Step

Take a moment to create your first grid using the first letter of a verse or passage you're currently memorizing or that you want to memorize. You can pull out notebook paper, an index card or take advantage of other free tools available in this book's additional resources.

More Bible Memory Resources

 Scan to find additional resources, including a downloadable PDF grid file and an online grid creation tool, or go to:

MemorizeWhatMatters.com/Resources

All Scripture is God-breathed and is useful for teaching, rebuking, correcting and training in righteousness.

2 Timothy 3:16

Chapter 2

Visual Outline Method

When I fly, I'm the person who prefers to book a window seat so I can look outside to get a glimpse of the crisscrossing web of roads, the beautiful geometric shapes of farmland and the tiny ant people who tend to think they're bigger than they actually are.

From thousands of feet up, I can scan hundreds of miles of terrain in seconds to understand how roads connect every city or town and how everything seems to bend to the shape of mountains, rivers, and lakes. I can understand so much from this altitude that even a map would not be able to communicate easily.

One of these days when I can muster up enough courage, I'm going to stick my head out of an airplane, locate a landing place down below, and jump. Lord willing, I'll have a parachute attached to my back when I do. While the parachute would unquestionably make the jump safe, it likely won't have any effect on the amount of screaming I'll do.

But I digress.

Memorizing Scripture is like memorizing the details of a map. Is it possible to simply reference the map instead of memorizing it? Of course. Can you memorize a map and still get lost? Absolutely. Is it possible to lose sight of the forest amid the trees? 100%.

I haven't gone into much detail about it in this book, I've spoken many time on the Bible Memory Goal YouTube channel[1] about the value of context when memorizing God's Word. We can miss a lot when we memorize a single verse, which is why I encourage people to at least try memorizing stories, chapters, or books of the Bible.

If we take even one step further back—or should I say if we float up to 30,000 feet—a different kind of value can be gained by seeing each book of the Bible as a whole.

---

1. Visit YouTube.com/@BibleMemoryGoal

For example, what if when somebody mentions Jesus walking on water, you automatically know that the story can be found in John chapter 6? You may not be able to recite the story word for word (yet), but you can flip immediately to it without a concordance or a search on your phone. Wouldn't that be amazing?

What if you were to hear a sermon on a section of John 17 and your mind immediately understands the context that everything Jesus prays is immediately preceding His arrest in chapter 18? Can you see how valuable that might be?

What if I told you that this kind of outline memorization of the Gospel of John could be accomplished in about 10 minutes? You might think I'm crazy, but I'm not. In this chapter, I'm going to give you a peek into what that process looks like, and by the end you'll know a highlight from each of the 21 chapters in John.

Let's get started!

There are multiple methods that can be used to memorize the structure or outline of a book, but the one I'll share with you here is a visual representation of each chapter number along with an associated story or idea from the chapter. There may be other themes or stories that get skipped, and if these are important to you, I encourage you to find a way to put your personal spin on the visual so that you can remember it.

Chapter 1. "In the beginning was the Word, and the Word was with God and the Word was God." The image you see is the shape of the number 1 with Word across the top and the Greek word θεὸς or theos, which means God.

Chapter 2. This is a visual representation of Jesus' first miracle turning water to wine at the wedding in Cana. You can see the shape of the number 2 dispensing wine into the many jars.

Chapter 3. "You must be born again." The number 3 resembles the shape of a pregnant woman, which can remind us of the conversation Jesus had with Nicodemus that includes the famous verse you've probably already memorized: John 3:16.

Chapter 4. Jesus meets the Samaritan woman at the well. This famous story is visualized by the number 4 that holds the drop line and bucket over the well.

Chapter 5. This is an image of the five porticos of the temple representing the fifth chapter. In this chapter, we have Jesus healing the invalid at the pool of

Bethesda and teaching in the temple, all under the shadow of these huge columns.

Chapter 6. Jesus feeds the 5,000 and then walks on water. This image shows the number 6 walking on water. If you'd like, you can also imagine that arms or legs of this number 6 are actually loaves and fish to remind you of both stories.

Chapter 7. Jesus celebrates the Feast of Tabernacles and teaches in the temple with some very skeptical religious leaders. The number 7 here looks very much like a flipped version of the F in *feasts*.

Chapter 8. This image depicts the story of Jesus and the woman caught in adultery who was about to be stoned by the Pharisees. The hourglass looks like a number 8 and also resemble a capital A, signifying where Jesus states His relationship with the Father definitively with multiple *I Am* statements, such as verse 58.

Chapter 9. Jesus heals the blind man by spitting in the dirt, creating mud, and putting it in his eyes. This whole chapter deals not only with physical blindness but also spiritual blindness. You can see how the number 9 is turned into an eye.

Chapter 10. Jesus speaks of being the Good Shepherd and of His people as His sheep. The number 10 is a visual of the door handle to the sheep pen, for which Jesus says He is the gatekeeper.

Chapter 11. This chapter contains the popular story of Jesus raising Lazarus from the dead. You can see both digits of the number 11 being covered in burial cloths and slowly coming back to life, just as Lazarus did in this chapter.

Chapter 12. Mary of Bethany pours out an expensive bottle of perfume to anoint Jesus' feet and wipe them with her hair. You can see how the number 2 here looks like a woman's flowing hair.

Chapter 13. Jesus washes his disciples' feet. You can see the number 1 on the pant leg, and the 3, which looks like a toe separator used during a pedicure.

Chapter 14. "I am the way, the truth and the life." This famous verse is visualized by a 1 and a 4, which look like crisscrossing roads that represent the way.

Chapter 15. "I am the vine and you are the branches." Jesus continues teaching his disciples with the metaphor of vines and branches, which make up both the 1 and the 5.

Chapter 16. Jesus comforts his confused disciples by telling them of the coming Spirit or Advocate. In this image, you can imagine the 1 as a tree trunk and the 6 as the nest for the dove representing the Holy Spirit.

Chapter 17. This entire chapter is known as Jesus' High Priestly Prayer when He prays both for his disciples and for all future believers—including you and me. Although not pictured, you can imagine the 1 as Jesus' arm, and you can see the 7 traces the outline of Jesus' praying hands.

Chapter 18. This chapter details Jesus' arrest and trial. The 8 in the 18 lends itself perfectly to resemble handcuffs. Were metal handcuffs likely used in Jesus' time? Probably not, but the image makes it easy to remember.

Chapter 19. We now move on to Jesus' death and burial. To remember this chapter, you can imagine the 1 as part of the cross and the 9 as Mary, Jesus' mother, mourning at the foot of the cross.

Chapter 20. This chapter tells us all about Jesus' resurrection. The tomb is empty! As you visualize this number, be sure that the 0 for the stone has already been rolled away, since this chapter is all about what happens *after* Jesus is resurrected.

Chapter 21. Jesus tells his disciples to fish on the other side of the boat, at which point they catch a lot of fish and recognize that the  resurrected Jesus is the one speaking. He then has breakfast with them on the shore and famously asks Peter 3 times (2+1) "Do you love me?"

While there may be some chapters that you need to review to remember, you'll be surprised at how easily you're able to build this kind of outline memory. You could also find a verse or two within each chapter that encapsulates what that chapter is about and start memorizing that as well, combining both the Outline and the Individual Verse memorization methods.

 Scan to download a larger version of these images that you can use to study along with other free Bible memory resources, or visit:

MemorizeWhatMatters.com/Resources

*Note: Special thanks to Dr. Larry Dinkins for the permission to use these images for the John outline. Learn more about his ministry here: www.oralstoryteller.org

How, then, can they call on the one they have not believed in? And how can they believe in the one of whom they have not heard? And how can they hear without someone preaching to them?

Romans 10:14

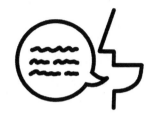

Chapter 3

Speak It Out Loud

W hat sounds good in our head doesn't always sound good when spoken aloud. This is true of ideas, foreign languages, and even bad dad jokes (not that I would know!).

If you have ever learned a second language, you know that there is a wide gap between those who study in a classroom and those who study on the streets of the country where that language is spoken daily.

During my time in China, foreign visitors or tourists who had studied Chinese in the classroom stood out like a McDonald's in Chinatown. Their accent was heavy, and the pacing of their speech was off. They had spent so much time trying to understand the mechanics of the grammar and various verb tenses, but without practicing it in daily conversation, that head knowledge rarely translated to smooth communication.

Those who studied for the same amount of time on the street and in daily life tended to have a less robust vocabulary and lacked proper grammar, but they communicated with ease and the language seemed to fit them like a well-tailored suit.

What was the difference? The primary difference was the connection being developed between the brain and the tongue.

This seems like such a simple concept, but this one strategy has changed the way I interact with God. When most people think about memorizing the Bible—or even reading it for that matter—they tend to imagine a scene in which a person is sitting quietly on a chair in a state of deep focus and meditation. We even have a name for this activity in the Christian world—quiet time.

The opposite is now true for me. When I read my Bible, I read it out loud. When I pray, I pray out loud. Can you guess what I do when I'm memorizing a passage of the Bible?

That's right. I recite it out loud.

One reason I do this is that it helps me focus. When I read in my head, it's far too easy for my mind to wander. Reading the passage aloud engages my mind, my mouth and my ears. This makes it harder, although not impossible, for my eyes to scan the page without registering the words.

When it comes to memorizing verses, stories, or passages in the Bible, however, there are some other compelling reasons to recite out loud. And when I say *out loud*, I don't mean whisper it under your breath or mumble it quickly. I mean *speak* it with conviction and authority.

Why?

Emotion Is a Memory Hook

It's unfortunate how often we lack emotion when reading God's Word. Usually, this is simply because we don't know which emotion to use, but when you memorize and meditate on a passage for weeks or months, it's hard not to feel some of the emotion present in the text. It could be the joy or despair of David in the psalms or the frustration or concern of Paul in one of his letters.

In the same way that writing a passage, making a flashcard, or creating an image or mnemonic can create a memory hook that helps you recall a verse, emotion also creates a memory hook.

When I recite Psalm 13 out loud, even when I'm by myself, the way that I resonate with David's deep feeling of abandonment is expressed in my voice. "How long, Lord? Will you forget me forever? How long will you hide your face from me?"

When I articulate the emotion as I recite, not only is the meaning of the passage fortified in my mind, it also becomes a hook that helps me recall what I've memorized. The words *how long* mournfully echo in my head as does David's request for God to *look on me and answer* (13:3).

The sooner you can recite passages you've memorized out loud, the better; and the sooner you can add emotion to your recitation, the stronger that memory will be.

Practice Using It

Using Scripture in everyday conversation may feel awkward to some or perhaps like it's the domain of super Christians. It's not.

In fact, speaking the truth of God's Word throughout the day is an incredibly rewarding part of memorizing it. In a world where religion is often scorned and ignored, you'd be surprised at how open people are to hearing the wisdom of the Bible.

There's a difference between saying, "I think" or "At church my pastor says" rather than something like, "You know, that reminds me of something I read in the Bible." Many times, I don't even let people know I'm quoting Scripture.

Thankfully, God is happy for us to plagiarize His Word. The author of Hebrews gives us an example of this when quoting Psalm 8 by saying "It has been testified somewhere..." (Hebrews 2:6 ESV) and on multiple occasions even Jesus simply says "It is written..." when quoting Scripture.[1]

When we review and meditate on God's Word by speaking it out loud, particularly the passages that we've memorized, we are practicing for that moment when the Holy Spirit presents an opportunity for us to use it in daily life.

---

1. Examples include: Matthew 4:4, Luke 19:46, John 6:45.

The more you do it, the easier it becomes and the more you will recognize the opportunities to speak a "a word fitly spoken" (Proverbs 25:11, KJV).

Whether you turn to the right or to the left, your ears will hear a voice behind you, saying, 'This is the way; walk in it.'

Isaiah 30:21

Chapter 4

Memorize Like an Actor

The Broadway smash hit *Hamilton* is well-known for its catchy hip-hop ballads that tell the story of U.S. founding father Alexander Hamilton during the Revolutionary War. It's a modern interpretation of history that is so engaging and entertaining, it's easy to overlook one of the most interesting facts about this play. The entire musical, which lasts about 3 hours, is packed with *20,520 words*.

For context, the average person speaks only 16,000 words throughout a single day. Even the gospel of Luke only has about 19,500 words (depending on the translation).

The actors in Hamilton are memorizing *a lot of words*.

How do they do it? What amazing techniques do actors use to learn hundreds of lines of text for their roles on stage and screen?

The truth is that the techniques actors use to memorize lines are as varied as the ones we're exploring here to memorize the Bible. Actors have their own methods that work best for them, and stage actors have the additional advantage of singing lines that often rhyme. But one aspect of what a stage actor has to do that we can learn from here is blocking and gesturing.

Blocking is a term that describes where actors stand on the stage and how they move. Gesturing is what they do with the rest of their body as they recite and interact with the other actors.

During rehearsals, these movements create hooks for the brain to place certain memories.

Every time an actor moves in a certain direction, she says a certain line.

Every time an actor reacts to a bit of dialogue, he throws up his hands and replies in exasperation.

While there is an art to reciting Scripture on stage—and I've met many people who have a passion for such a practice—most of us won't ever find ourselves performing what we've memorized in front of a large crowd. That doesn't mean, however, that we can't take cues from how actors use movement as part of their memory process.

Let's take a moment to explore some ways we can use movement as we memorize God's Word.

Incorporate Hand Motions

Hand motions are not just for children's church. It may feel a bit awkward to start using body movements if you've never done it before, but when you combine physical body movement with brain exercise, memories tend to stick.

This isn't movement for the sake of movement, though. You want the actions of your arms and hands to represent the words or feelings of the verse you're reciting. For example, when I review Galatians 4:19–20, my face contorts in pain as I clinch my fists and then my left hand goes up to my forehead in an act of perplexity.

"My dear children, for whom I am again in the *pains* of childbirth until Christ is formed in you, how I wish I could be with you now and change my tone, but I am *perplexed* about you!"

I also find a lot of value in pointing or counting off my fingers when reciting a list of things or ideas in a passage. Sometimes I can associate the list item with the number of fingers or where I'm pointing, but more often than not it simply helps me not to skip or forget a listed item.

I'll use James 3:7 to illustrate this point. "All kinds of animals, birds, reptiles and sea creatures are being tamed and have been tamed by mankind." Using my left hand, starting with my pointer finger down to my pinky, I can list each of these off easily. As it so happens, this corresponds well with the position of each category of God's creation on the earth.

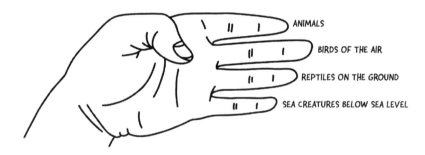

- **Pointer finger**—overarching category of animals

- **Middle finger**—birds of the air

- **Ring finger**—reptiles on the ground level

- **Pinky finger**—sea creatures below sea level

Be creative with how you use your hands and remember that it only needs to make sense to you. If you need help creating meaning with your hands, though, you can also consider sign language.

Sign Language

Hands have been used to create meaning and express ideas for hundreds of years in the form of sign language. There's no reason to reinvent the wheel.

You don't have to learn every word of a verse or passage with sign language (unless you want to). For me, I tend to use sign language for those words or phrases that I find particularly hard to remember. For example, throughout the short book of Philemon, Paul and Timothy often refer to Jesus as Christ or Christ Jesus, so I found that I always messed up verse 5. "Because I hear about your love for all his holy people and your faith in the Lord Jesus."

In this case, it helps me to physically sign the word *Lord,* which is an L (extended first finger and thumb) moving from one shoulder to the opposite hip to indicate a sash, followed by the sign for *Jesus,* which is touching each middle finger into the palm of the opposite hand to indicate the nail marks.

Every time I recite this verse within Philemon, I'm either thinking about this sign language or I'm physically acting it out with my hands. In both cases, I'm using physical movement as a peg to remember to say *Lord Jesus.*

If you don't know how to sign a certain word, there's an amazing visual database of vocabulary you can browse on the American Sign Language University YouTube channel.[1]

Body Movement

In the same way that blocking helps actors know where to be and move within a scene, we can include a type of blocking in our memorization of Scripture.

Take a step forward; take a step backward; turn your body to the left or to the right. The movements don't need to take up a lot of space as long as they are specific and connected to the passage in some way.

You can also walk a specific path every time you recite a certain verse or passage of the Bible. Over time, your mind

---

1. YouTube.com/@aslu

will begin to associate words or parts of Scripture with the location that you tend to pass every time you recite.

I've talked a lot on the Memorize What Matters podcast about how I love to recite Scripture while I walk my dog. My dog Lexi and I love routine, so we tend to walk the exact same path every morning and evening. The walk takes us about 15 minutes, which just so happens to be the amount of time it takes me to recite all of 2 Timothy, among other short epistles.

The more that I've reviewed 2 Timothy during the walk, the more that my mind has started to associate particular corners or houses as the starting point for a chapter or verse. In a way, I'm passively building a mind palace, also called a memory palace (which we'll discuss in Chapter 10, Mind Palace) by allowing my mind to make associations between my surroundings and my recitation.

Combine the Movements

Ultimately, the movements you decide to use are limited only by your imagination and creativity. You can focus on just one kind of movement, or you can incorporate all three.

One of my favorite examples of this comes from Isaiah 30:21. "Whether you turn to the right or to the left, your ears will hear a voice behind you, saying, 'This is the way; walk in it.'"

Instead of repeating this verse over and over to memorize, it's much easier to remember if you physically turn your body to the right and to the left (body movement), cup your hands behind your ears (hand motion) and then point both palms forward in front of you (sign language for *way*).

You've linked body movement to the words and meaning of a verse in a way that makes it much harder to forget.

These commandments that I give you today are to be on your hearts. Impress them on your children. Talk about them when you sit at home and when you walk along the road, when you lie down and when you get up. Tie them as symbols on your hands and bind them on your foreheads. Write them on the doorframes of your houses and on your gates.

Deuteronomy 6:6–9

Chapter 5

Write Them on the Doorframes

What people hang on the walls of their homes reflects what they value, the things that they want to be reminded of every time they enter a room. Usually, these hangings consist of family portraits, wedding photos, art pieces, or photography from a beautiful vacation memory. Sometimes, people have a plaque or mural with a Scripture verse written on it.

As beautiful and decorative as these reminders are, over time they eventually blend in with the surroundings. For me, it often takes a guest to come into my home and comment on a painting or photo on my wall to prompt me to see it again.

Contrast that with my refrigerator door. The items on the refrigerator door seem to constantly change day by day, and I'm forced to look at them every time I want to grab a snack or a drink. Whether it's my son's latest test score, an invitation we've received, or a Christmas card photo, this tiny billboard in our home gets lots of attention.

Hanging Scripture in our home is about more than finding a beautiful piece of art that has a verse printed on it. It's about finding creative ways to display Bible verses that can also grab our attention. We put it in places we simply can't ignore.

What works may be different for each of us, but here are a few hanging ideas I've used or heard about from others:

- **Mobile Phone Lock Screen.** I've heard estimates that people take out their phones an average of 144 times per day. That's crazy! Although it might only be a momentary glance, having a lock screen image with the verse you're currently memorizing can be a great daily review. You could even turn off Face ID (the feature that automatically unlocks your phone by scanning your face) and set a rule for yourself that you have to recite the verse once before you can open your phone. Not only will you recite your verse so many more times throughout the day, but it might also have the side benefit of discouraging you from mindlessly opening your phone for no reason.

- **Writing on a Mirror, Window, or Whiteboard.** Write your current memory verse on your bathroom mirror or the big glass sliding door that leads to your backyard. Maybe you have a prominent whiteboard for family messages to write on. Whatever you choose, writing down a Bible verse using a dry erase marker on a glass surface is a fun way to display the verse for yourself or for your family. As a bonus, you can easily erase a word or two each day as you review to test how well you've memorized the verse. By the end of the week, every word can be erased, indicating a completed verse and allowing you to start with a new verse.

- **Laminated Sheet in the Shower.** Print out a list of Bible verses that you want to memorize or review and laminate it. Hang this laminated list of verses in the shower so that you can see it easily every morning or evening as you bathe.

- **Sticky Notes or Index Cards.** Write out the verse reference on one side of an index card or sticky note and, if you like, write out the whole verse on the back side. You can then place the sticky note anywhere you know you'll have to see it, such as the dashboard of your car, your jewelry box, or the coffee maker.

- **Dedicated Peg Board**. In our home, we have a dedicated board with a cord draped from side to side. We clip our index cards to this cord using a wooden clothes pin to keep all the verses that our family is currently memorizing. Our peg board is the first thing people see when entering our home.

Displaying the verses you want to memorize and writing them "on the doorframes of your houses" as we read in Deuteronomy, is an effective strategy, but if you're not careful, these visual reminders can quickly become another decoration that you start to ignore as it becomes part of your everyday surroundings.

One way to combat this is to constantly change the verses that you display on your phone or that you write on the mirror. Another option is to take advantage of a technique I call *spaced stacking*.

Spaced Stacking

In his book *Atomic Habits*, James Clear describes a well-known psychological technique called habit stacking. Instead of trying to use willpower to create a new habit, the idea is to identify a current habit that I already do and stack a new behavior on top of it. By linking a new habit to one that I already have established, I make it more likely that I'll actually complete both tasks.

This can easily be applied to Bible memory, even using some of the hanging techniques mentioned in the last section.

- While I'm brushing my teeth, I recite the verse I have written on my mirror.

- While I'm showering, I recite the day's verses.

- Before I pour a cup of coffee, I say the verse on the notecard.

In each case, I found something I do every day and attached my verse review to that habit. It's not simply a reminder, it's an action I have to take.

You can take this a step further by combining spaced repetition (see Chapter 11, Spaced Repetition) with habit stacking to form what I call *spaced stacking*.

Spaced stacking leverages the power of habits that we do at different intervals to help us review over longer and longer periods of time. For example, I walk my dog every day in the morning, but I only mow my lawn once a week. I make coffee every morning, but I pay my water bill monthly.

Using these examples, my spaced stacking process can look like this:

- Every day when I walk my dog, I recite verses I need to review daily.

- Every week when I mow my lawn, I recite the verses that I moved to a weekly review.

- Every month when I pay my water bill, I will stop to recite a set of verses that have been designated for monthly review.

You can keep track of these daily, weekly, and monthly reviews manually or digitally, but the idea is that by attaching them to an action that you do consistently at those intervals, you won't forget to review.

Put It into Practice

Make a list of the activities or habits that you do on a daily, weekly, and monthly basis. Circle the ones that could easily be combined with reviewing verses and brainstorm which of the ideas listed above (for example, phone lock screen, sticky notes, peg board) would trigger a reminder to stack those habits.

Hear the word of the Lord, you descendants of Jacob, all you clans of Israel. This is what the Lord says...

Jeremiah 2:4–5a

Chapter 6
Record and Listen

M y son was only two years old when we sat on the bed one evening to read a bedtime story. He requested his favorite book, one that I'm sure I had read to him at least 100 times in the past year.

But this time was different. My son had a surprise for me.

I was halfway through the first page when Josiah stopped me, taking the book from my hands. To my shock, he started reading the words with 100% accuracy and flipping the pages as he went. *My son is a prodigy! He's reading at only 2 years old!*

As I was in the middle of mentally writing my acceptance speech for the inevitable Dad of the Year award that was coming my way, I noticed that Josiah forgot to turn to the next page. He continued to read the words from the next page without having flipped the page.

I realized what I'm sure many parents have experienced before. My son wasn't reading as much as he was reciting what he had unintentionally memorized from having heard me read it thousands of times. (Did I say hundreds before? It was a *lot.*). He even mimicked the same voices and vocal inflections that I made when I read that book.

Kids are incredible listeners. So good, in fact, that they often hear things we wish they hadn't. We incorrectly assume that we lose this skill as we get older, but we don't. Listening is still as powerful as it was when we were younger, it simply requires us to be more intentional about how we do it.

Redeem the Time

Author Glenna Marshall calls it "redeeming the time" when she makes use of the moments in her day when her hands are busy but her mind is not. Washing the dishes. Running errands. Jogging or walking for exercise.

Usually, we put on a music playlist, a podcast, or (if you're old school) the radio to fill that dead time, but this is a perfect opportunity to redeem what sometimes gets wasted. Listening to the verses or passages that you've memorized is surprisingly effective at solidifying a memory in your brain.

Yes, there are audio Bibles available, and I know how soothing it is to listen to a professional actor with a rich, deep voice narrate the words of Scripture.

While this certainly is an option for listening to the Bible, over the years I've discovered that making my own audio recording is much better for memorizing God's Word. Why?

- **Custom Verse Groupings.** Instead of having to skip through a professional audio recording to find the specific verse you memorized, making your own recording allows you to create a personalized collection of Bible verses or passages that reflects exactly what you're memorizing.

- **Unique Vocal Inflection.** Each of us has a unique way of emphasizing or pronouncing words in a sentence. Recording your own voice allows you to insert your own tone and emotion into the passage, which as we learned is a memory hook itself.

* **It's Translation Neutral.** Sometimes it's hard to find an audio Bible in the translation you prefer to memorize. Recording your own audio file gives you the flexibility to choose whichever translation or language works best for you.

Thankfully, producing this kind of digital recording has become very easy. Every mobile device you keep in your pocket—iPhone or Android—comes with a voice memo app you can use to record the verses you're memorizing.

Sit down one day this week and knock out a few recordings. You can create one that's a minute or less for the moments when you just want a quick review and another that's 5 to 10 minutes for those parts in your day that allow for more time.

Audio Recording Tips

Let me share with you a few tips that I've learned myself or been introduced to.

- **Read, Don't Recite.** If you listen to an audio file that has errors, you're going to adopt those errors into your memory. You'll want to make sure that the recording you listen to is accurate. It's best to record yourself *reading* the verses instead of reciting them from memory.

- **Use a Looping App.** Looping apps are designed for musicians to loop a particular melody for practice, but they are also excellent at allowing you to put a verse you want to memorize on repeat. Whereas most voice recording apps on your phone don't allow you to repeat without pressing play again, apps such as Jam Looper (iOS) or Loopify (Android) let you put a verse or collection of verses on repeat forever.

- **Speak with a Recording.** When I'm listening to my Scripture recordings while driving to the store or running, the best way I stay engaged with the recording (rather than letting my mind wander) is to speak the memorized passage along with the recording. It's not always easy to do, but it's a fun challenge.

Take the Next Step

Pull out your Bible and your phone. Open the voice recorder app and record yourself reading the verses that you're currently memorizing. If you want to memorize the verse reference, be sure to read that during the recording as well.

And Moses recited the words of this song from beginning to end in the hearing of the whole assembly of Israel.

Deuteronomy 31:30

Chapter 7

Sing the Bible

W hy is it that we can remember the lyrics to a song from decades ago and then forget where we put our keys earlier this morning?

This phenomenon holds true whether or not you're musically inclined or even whether the song in question was on your regular playlist. We don't memorize music, we experience it, and because of this, the connection we have with music often transcends short-term or long-term memory.

As a musician myself, I'm fascinated by the emotional affect music has on my psyche. When I exercise, turning on upbeat, inspirational songs genuinely makes me run faster. When I'm sad, there's something about the simple sound of

Yo-Yo Ma's bow hitting the strings of a cello that comforts me, often to the point of tears.

Music is more than a collection of tones arranged in the form of a melody. I believe that God designed music to speak the language of our souls, and it's one reason why music seems to be an integral part of our upcoming heavenly experience (Revelation 5:8–9, 14:2–3, 15:2–4).

The psalms of the Bible were originally set to music and, considering the broad spectrum of emotions that the psalms exemplify, it stands to reason that the original music reflected the emotions in some way. Modern artists have done an amazing job re-imagining what that might have sounded like using instruments and melodies that fit our current tastes.

Considering music's ability to connect with our emotions and memory, it would be crazy not to harness its power to help us memorize more of the Bible. If you grew up in Sunday school, you might remember a few Scripture songs that were sung at church with catchy tunes that stick like crazy glue to your brain.

Thankfully, technology gives us access to all sorts of amazing Scripture music that we can now use as adults to improve our retention of the Bible verses we're trying to memorize. Once you find or create a song that follows your preferred translation, put it on repeat and start singing along.

Here are a few ideas to consider:

Online Music Resources

Thanks to the ubiquity of platforms like YouTube, Spotify, Apple Music, and others, it's surprisingly easy to find almost any popular Scripture passage sung in many different translations. If you already have an idea of which verses you want to memorize, simply search for "[book] + [translation] + song" (for example, Colossians ESV song) on YouTube to see what's available.

Another approach is to find a group or artist that you like and binge the songs they've made available. For example:

* **Slugs and Bugs.** This group produces excellent kids' music. Their *Sing the Bible* series is amazing. My young boys can recite all the books of the Bible thanks to their "Old Testament Song" and "New Testament Song," both of which are so catchy that even adults enjoy it.

- **The Corner Room.** If you're looking for more mature melodies that you could easily add to your worship playlist, The Corner Room has published a beautiful collection of songs you'll love.

- **Shane & Shane.** This popular Christian duo has put many of the psalms to music, but it's their *Worship in the Word* album, written with kids in mind, which makes Scripture so easy to sing.

- **The Bible Song.** Bible Song, a ministry of Word4Word Ministries, aims to put the entire Bible to music and already has a stunning library of entire chapters and books of the Bible.

There are so many other examples that I could list here, both professional and amateur, that fit every imaginable musical taste or Biblical translation.

Scan for a more comprehensive list of music resources, or visit:

MemorizeWhatMatters.com/Scripture-Music

AI-Created Music Resources

Technology is now at a place where artificial intelligence (AI) can create custom music using whatever style and lyrics you request. It doesn't matter if you prefer rap, country, bluegrass, or gospel music, AI is surprisingly good at producing legitimate melodies in a matter of minutes.

The landscape of AI startups is changing so rapidly right now that it won't do any good for me to try to predict which tools will be available months or years from the moment I'm writing. Perhaps one particular tool will emerge as *the* AI music creation tool. In the meantime, you can search for some phrase such as *AI music maker tool* to see what's available.

The tools I've used allow me to type out the exact text I would like to be used as lyrics and then use words to describe the style of music, such as "in the style of a country ballad" or "in the style of an old gospel music song."

In my experience, these AI tools work best with individual verses (rather than long passages), and the quality of the final product is hit or miss. I don't believe these tools will replace the creativity of the human artists listed above, but if you want to memorize a more obscure translation and there aren't any existing music resources available online, AI is a worth a try.

Curious what this kind of AI music sounds like? Scan to hear the variety of genres that I was able to create with AI, or you can visit:

MemorizeWhatMatters.com/AI-music

Write Your Own Music

Are you thinking, *Yeah right. I have a hard time writing an email much less a Scripture song, I can't do that.* But that's not true.

Being an experienced musician is less important than you might think when it comes to writing your own Scripture music. Nobody has to hear these songs except you, and the process of creating the song serves as a memory hook for the verses you want to internalize.

Sit down with your instrument, your Bible, and a phone to record the song. Try to build a simple melody and fit the words in whatever way you can. Don't worry—it likely won't rhyme and the recording won't be radio quality. The purpose is to have fun while using the creative gifts God has given you to sing his Word as an act of worship.

My son, do not forget my teaching, but keep my commands in your heart, for they will prolong your life many years and bring you peace and prosperity. Let love and faithfulness never leave you; bind them around your neck, write them on the tablet of your heart.

Proverbs 3:1–3

Chapter 8

Print the Page and Mark It Up

"**B**ring me your Bible." As weird as the request seemed, when two Chinese police officers were standing at my apartment door telling me to get my Bible, that's exactly what I did.

I started walking back to my bedroom, wondering what in the world they wanted with my Bible. For the last week, I had been picked up every morning and driven to an interrogation facility to face my next round of questioning. It was clear they thought I was a spy, but they were also very much aware that I was a Christian who was not shy about my faith. Being a follower of Jesus in China isn't technically illegal, but talking about it with others is a gray area.

I emerged from my bedroom with my Bible and handed it to one of the police officers. Without hesitation, he opened the book and started flipping through it. A scowl slowly appeared on his face.

"Where's your real Bible?"

"My real Bible?" I was genuinely confused.

"Yes, this Bible has no writing in it. No marking or highlighting. We need your real Bible."

He was right. Up until that point, I wasn't the kind of person who liked to write in my Bible. It felt so permanent, especially when my thoughts on a certain passage might evolve over time.

"I don't write in my Bible," I mumbled, still caught off guard by the fact that such a stereotype existed, not to mention the fact that I didn't fit it. The officer was visibly unhappy with my answer, but he chose to let it go.

A moment of silence went by. Finally, after thinking it over, he looked up at me. "Come with us."

For the next half hour, we meandered through the city in an unmarked car without a word spoken. The officer held my Bible in his lap as if it were evidence in a trial. When we finally reached our destination, I was led into a room and seated in a chair facing my accusers. My primary interrogator took the Bible from the officer's hand and did something that I never would have anticipated and never will forget.

He walked up to me and held out the Bible. "Put your hand on your Bible."

We were not in a court and China is not a Christian country, so I couldn't figure out what was going on.

"Hold your other hand up," he said. "I'm going to ask you questions now. And since you're a Christian, if you lie with your hand on the Bible, you'll go to hell. That's what you believe, right?"

His theology was questionable, but it didn't seem like now was the right time to correct him.

"Okay." With my right hand on the Bible and my left hand held in the air, I waited. I felt like I was in an old courtroom drama show, but this situation was very real.

He began. "Do you swear that you are not a spy of the U.S. government?"

In the years since this crazy—and absolutely true—incident, my attitude toward writing in my Bible has changed. However, the catalyst for this change had less to do with these Chinese police and more to do with me prioritizing Bible memory.

As I read and study through the Bible, I love finding connections in the passage with something I've memorized elsewhere and writing that down as my own cross-reference. In fact, I purchased a journaling Bible that had enough space on the sides for the express purpose of making these kinds of notes without writing over the biblical text.

I know many people who have an incredible, elaborate system for highlighting, underlining, and marking in their Bibles. That's still not me, but if that's you, go for it.

During one interview on the Memorize What Matters podcast, I spoke with pastor and best-selling author Levi Lusko, who shared with me a brilliant idea that I've adopted for my own use. When he's memorizing a chapter of the Bible, he photocopies that page of his Bible, laminates it,[1] and brings it with him to review throughout the day.

This works especially well if you're memorizing an extended passage of Scripture, but the method can be

---

1. Most of us don't own laminating machines, but thankfully online retailers and most office supply stores sell self-adhesive laminating sheets that work well for this purpose.

applied even with a collection of individual verses printed on a sheet of paper.

I have found incredible benefits to this photocopy technique.

Spatial Tracking

Brains have a special knack for spatial awareness—the ability to remember physical spaces such as the house we grew up in, the park we loved to visit as a kid, or even the grocery store we visit every week. We're going to dive deeper into this mental superpower in a later chapter, but for now it's important to note that the placement of words and verses on a physical page can also act as a hook for our memory.

It could be the position of the verse on the left side of the page rather than on the right side, which column it's in, or even where the line break happens in a sentence. The location of the words can help your memory navigate the passage in your mind as you memorize and review.

This same kind of spatial tracking doesn't exist when scrolling through a digital Bible, which is one of the reasons why I recommend prioritizing a physical Bible over a digital Bible when memorizing Scripture.

Easy Transport

Carrying around a physical Bible everywhere you go throughout the day isn't always practical. Sure, you could open your phone to use it, but that opens the door to distraction in the form of other notifications and apps awaiting you.

A photocopy of the page or part of a page from your Bible is a perfect compromise that is both portable and convenient. Keep it in your back pocket and start making a habit of pulling it out when you're in an elevator, on public transport, or anywhere you can safely look at it and recite your passage.

Guilt-Free Marking

While I'm hesitant to mark up my actual Bible, as you know, I have no problem marking up a photocopy. Effective ways of marking the text to help with Bible memory include the following ideas

- Highlight the words that you have a difficult time

remembering.

- Use different color highlighters for specific words or names. For example, *Jesus* could always be highlighted in red throughout a passage.

- Underline letters where you can see a mnemonic pattern (see Chapter 9, Puzzle Patterns, for more on mnemonics).

- Draw little pictures to help you remember a phrase.

- Circle names you have a hard time pronouncing.

Each of these, as simple as they seem, can create a much-needed hook to help you remember words in a verse or passage.

Custom Verse Collections

When working with topical collections of verses (see What's Your P.O.I.N.T.?), gathering all of the verses onto a single printed page can provide clarity and convenience. It can be helpful to have all the verses together to see how they relate to one another. In other cases, it helps to maintain a certain order.

For example, the Romans Road verses tell the story of sin and redemption. Preserving the verse sequence on a printed page will help you when memorizing and reviewing and then telling the story effectively.

Even when the order is inconsequential, spatial awareness of where the verses are on the page is a memory tool that you won't fully appreciate until you use it.

The secret things belong to the Lord our God, but the things revealed belong to us and to our children forever, that we may follow all the words of this law.

Deuteronomy 29:29

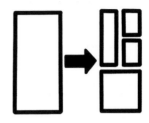

Chapter 9

Puzzle Patterns

I have a love-hate relationship with jigsaw puzzles. The problem isn't the puzzle itself; I actually love to put together a puzzle. The problem is that I can't stand to have an unfinished puzzle. If you know anything about puzzles larger than 1,000 pieces, you know that it's not something you can finish in a short amount of time.

Sometimes during the holiday breaks, my family will start on a puzzle, and we'll get all four of us around the table working to find where each piece fits. Then, after about 30 minutes my two young boys will get bored and find something more fun to do. My wife will work on it for a couple hours with me but eventually take a break. As for me, I have what probably borders on an unhealthy obsession to get it finished.

The world record for finishing a 1,000 piece puzzle is 1 hour and 40 minutes.[1] I'm nowhere close to that fast, but I have learned that there are certain techniques you can use to make things go faster. The obvious one is to take time to put all the pieces right side up. After this, the most common technique used by puzzlers is to group puzzle pieces by either shape or color. We all usually do something similar when we group together the end pieces to form the border of the puzzle.

With the pieces grouped by certain patterns, it's much easier to see a hole in the puzzle and then retrieve the necessary piece to complete the picture.

Our brain works in much the same way. For most of us, our memories are pieces of a puzzle scattered around a table: some right side up, some upside down, and none of them organized in any way. Trying to recall a memory is often like finding that one piece of the puzzle. You know it's there and you have an idea of what it should look like, but it's lost in a mess of other memories.

---

1. MemorizeWhatMatters.com/puzzle-record

Similar to a puzzle, though, it's possible to group together information to make the storage and retrieval of our memories much easier. In the memory world, words such as *chunking* and *clustering* describe this process, but for the purpose of memorizing the Bible, it'll be easier to give you a few examples of how this might work.

The Power of Lists

The easiest place to find memory groupings when memorizing the Bible is with lists. For example, when Paul says that he was "appointed a herald and an apostle and a teacher" in 2 Timothy 1:11, it's easy to forget the words or get them out of order. However, by grouping the key words in the list together, you get this:

Herald

Apostle

Teacher

A hat. It just so happens that you put a hat on your hair, which helps me remember that it all starts with *hair-ald*.

Another great example is memorizing the list of the 12 disciples. Various jingles and great rhymes have been written to help with memorizing the names, or if you like, you could group the information into a different visual: Imagine Jesus drinking a steaming hot cup of *tea* with his disciples, making a *peanut butter and jelly (PB&J)* sandwich for each of them and then instead of turning water into wine, He turns a can of *Spam*—that fake meat in a can—into juicy, well-cooked steaks. Now that's a miracle that I'd love to see!

Thomas

Philip
Bartholomew
James, James, Jude, Judas, John

Simon
Peter
Andrew
Matthew

The problem most people have with finding or creating these imaginary patterns is that it takes quite a bit of creative energy. Thankfully, there are other ways of grouping words or phrases that aren't quite as brain intensive.

Breaking it Down

The way you group information doesn't need to be complex. In fact, sometimes breaking it down into simple, smaller groups of information works best. We do this with phone numbers all the time. Instead of trying to remember a string of 10 digits, we usually split them up into groups of three and four digits.

You can create these same easily digestible phrases when you want to memorize a Bible verse as well. For example, compare the difference between Psalm 1:1 in sentence form and written out in shorter phrases. First, let's see the verse as a single sentence:

"Blessed is the one who does not walk in step with the wicked or stand in the way that sinners take or sit in the company of mockers."

Now see this same verse broken up into shorter phrases:

"Blessed is the one
who does not walk
in step with the wicked
or stand in the way
that sinners take
or sit in the company
of mockers."

These shorter phrases are more manageable and at least feel easier to memorize. The psalms lend themselves well to phrase groupings as do proverbs with the various opposite and similar parallel statements. Write out the text in your notebook or print it on a sheet of paper.

We can take this a step further, though, with an example from the New Testament. Both Paul and Peter, the authors of many epistles, are known for their long, run-on sentences. When I was memorizing the introduction to 1 Peter, the second verse felt like one long sentence, the kind that I always had to diagram in English class during my elementary school years: "who have been chosen according to the foreknowledge of God the Father, through the sanctifying work of the Spirit, to be obedient to Jesus Christ and sprinkled with his blood."

To organize and group this information, the first step I took was to break it down into more manageable phrases. In this case, Peter describes his intended audience in four ways:

1 — Who have been chosen according to the foreknowledge of God the Father
2 – through the sanctifying work of the Spirit
3 – to be obedient to Jesus Christ
4 – and sprinkled with his blood

Again, this process of breaking the verse down into smaller phrases can make it slightly easier to visualize and thus memorize. To build on this method, however, the next step is to search for specific words or phrases that create a noticeable pattern. When I look at this verse, I see the key words *foreknowledge, sanctifying, obedient,* and *sprinkled* as the primary hooks I would want to remember from each phrase. Various Bible memorizers could think of hundreds of creative ways to incorporate these words into an image; I imagine somebody yelling "fore!" while playing golf on a deserted island where he spells *SOS* to get rescued.

Fore = foreknowledge

S = sanctifying

O = obedient

S = sprinkled

The more unique and personal the image, the more likely you are to remember it. This is one way to work with phrase or word groupings, but it also highlights another important technique that I love using more than anything else.

First Letters...Supercharged!

The method of using the first letter from a list or sentence of words to create a memorable pattern is something we've probably all done at some point in our lives. Do you remember the colors of the rainbow? For many people, the first thing that comes to mind is ROY-G-BIV (red, orange, yellow, green, blue, indigo, violet).

What about the order of the planets in our solar system? Many kids are taught a phrase similar to My Very Educated Mother Just Served Us Nachos (Mercury, Venus, Earth, Mars, Jupiter, Saturn, Uranus, Neptune).

It doesn't matter if you use an acrostic or an acronym—or if you even know the difference! The best way to apply this Bible memory approach is to begin with the first letter technique described in Chapter 1, First Letter Method. Seeing the first letters by themselves helps you see whether any words or patterns naturally stand out. I find that it's particularly helpful when looking at a list of names, places, or character qualities in the passage.

For example, in the first verse of 1 Peter, the provinces of Pontus, Galatia, Cappadocia, Asia, and Bithynia become "P G C A a B." While it might usually be difficult to remember these provinces and what order they are listed, imagining a PG movie about a yellow *cab* could potentially make that easier.

In James chapter 1 (ESV), the author reminds us that "Every good gift and every perfect gift is from above." Writing this out using the first-letter method, you get the following:

Eggaepgifa

Notice anything at the beginning of that phrase? I don't know about you, but the first thing I see is an *Egg*. Sometimes all it takes is the first few words of a verse to get me started, and remembering an *egg* falling from *above* is all I need to begin reciting this verse.

In both examples, the pattern isn't evident until the first letter of each word is written out and examined as a group. This can be done when you first start to memorize a new verse by quickly writing out the first letters of the words in the verse and seeing what you discover. It could also be used as a supplementary technique when you've already memorized a verse but continually stumble over a certain word or phrase. Looking at the first letters of that word or phrase within the context of surrounding words in the verse might help you tie it all together.

Going back to the earlier analogy, we're organizing the pieces of the memory puzzle in order to make the jumble of words and verses easier to memorize or recall. It may sound complex, but the more you practice the technique, the faster you'll be able to recognize these grouping patterns.

At the end of the day, we're just trying to find creative, visual ways to anchor the text of the Bible to our memory. In the next chapter, we're going to take this to the extreme with a strategy that has been used for thousands of years by everybody from Aristotle to modern memory champions.

Do not let your hearts be troubled. You believe in God; believe also in me. My Father's house has many rooms; if that were not so, would I have told you that I am going there to prepare a place for you?

John 14:1–2

Chapter 10
Mind Palace

"**G** et out!"

He pointed to the man and woman sitting in the corner of the room.

The woman, shocked by the odd request, could only a manage a simple "What?" before he spoke again.

"Get out! I need to go to my mind palace." This Sherlock Holmes character, portrayed by actor Benedict Cumberbatch, may have seemed certifiably mad, but few would ever be brave enough to deny such a stern request.

"Your what?" the lady stammers again. This time, the man sitting next to her, Dr. Watson, calmly grabs his coat, begins to escort her out of the room, and explains what's going on.

"A mind palace," he says. "It's a sort of memory technique, a mental map. You plot a map with a location—it doesn't have to be a real place—and then you deposit memories there. Theoretically, you can never forget anything. All you have to do is find your way back to it."

Then, as only Sherlock Homes can do, he sits in silence while piecing together clues, solving a mystery that has perplexed even the smartest investigators.

The general perception of the Mind Palace memory technique, as perpetuated in the scene from the BBC TV series *Sherlock*, is that it's only available to those with a high IQ.

Studies in neuroscience have proven, however, that even regular people who learn and apply this memory technique develop certain brain patterns that resemble those of professional memory athletes. In other words, you—yes, even you—can take advantage of this incredible method to improve your memory.

Entire books have been written about the Mind Palace method; I'm only going to be able to scratch the surface here in a single chapter, but to help you understand this technique as best I can, we're going to look at it from three angles: the premise, the process, and the biblical application.

The Premise Behind the Technique

The foundational premise of the Mind Palace method rests on our brain's incredible spatial awareness. Take a moment to think back to your childhood home. In your mind's eye, stand on the street in front of the house and then walk through the front door. Navigate the entryway and through the hallway until you reach your old bedroom. Look around for a moment.

What did you see on the walls? How was the furniture arranged? Where is the window and the closet door in your childhood bedroom?

Chances are you've surprised yourself by how much detail you can remember. God has designed our brains to understand and recall the places we visit frequently with incredible detail.

The premise of the Mind Palace method is establishing a space you know very well and can't easily forget—your childhood home, the office where you work every day, the neighborhood grocery store—and attaching abstract information to locations within that space. You'll find two distinct advantages to doing this.

Linking new information to deep memories gives your brain a place to put the new memory. This is a memory hook I've referenced throughout this book. It creates a kind of filing system for your brain so it can systematically encode and recall the information rather than scattering it like pages on the ground.

A mind palace also provides order and points of recall for your memory. With Bible memorization specifically, rote memorization (that is, repeating a passage over and over) is very linear by nature. You're building words and verses on top of each other like a stack of Jenga blocks. When you remove a single block, all the others can tumble down. If your mind goes blank on a particular word or verse, all the following verses fall too. A mind palace, on the other hand, gives you a new location for each verse or passage you're memorizing so that you can more easily navigate the passage even if you trip up on one word or verse.

That's what the mind palace is. Let me describe how it works in practice.

The Process of Building a Mind Palace

We're going to break down the process of building a mind palace into three parts: choosing the palace, dividing the space, and encoding the memory.

The best palace is an actual location that you know well. I've used my home where I grew up, the church building of my childhood, my current home, and even the streets in my neighborhood as a mind palace for various portions of Scripture. It's possible to create imaginary palaces, but when you're starting out, it's best to start with an actual location that you know well.

As you're learning the basics of this technique, consider using a single room in your home or office. Choose a room that has plenty of furniture, decorations, and other items that can be used for individual locations.

For the sake of this exercise, divide the room into 11 distinct locations. I recommend you start at the door of the room and walk around in a clockwise direction, picking items or places that stick out to you. For example, I would pick the door as Location 1 and then the little cabinet by the door as Location 2. Continue to work your way through the room, picking things like lamps, hanging pictures, a trash bin, a desk. If you do this exercise mentally, write down each location and its numeric position in a notebook. In the past, I've done this process while standing in the actual room, writing the number on a notecard, and taping it to the location.

When you're finished, you'll have 11 locations spread around the entire room. Test yourself to see if you can close your eyes and point out each location in your mind as if you were standing at the door of the room.

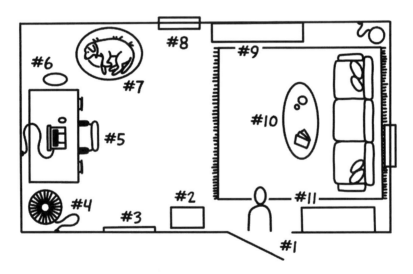

Congratulations! You've just created a mind palace.

There are so many additional skills and techniques to using a mind palace that are beyond the scope of what I can cover here, but keep in mind that there's no right way to create a palace. Build and modify in a way that suits your needs and the type of memorization you're doing.

The final part of the Mind Palace process is encoding the memory. This is where the technique is put to the test. The key to this part of the process is to simplify what you want to memorize into the most basic image or idea and then glue that image to the location.

Let's start with something that's already simple, a grocery list.

If you want to remember a list of groceries you need to buy when you go to the store, you could put each of the items on a location in your palace. The simple image would be the item itself, eggs, cheese, coffee, or bread.

The glue is an interaction that happens between the grocery item and the location that will help your mind remember that this image goes with a specific location. In this case, I could take an oversized egg—imagine an ostrich egg—and throw it against my Location 1, my door. I imagine the yellow yolk of that egg dripping down the door and making a puddle on the floor below it.

Next, I can put a slice of cheese to cover the entire top of the side table next to the door, which is my Location 2. The holes in the cheese might be where I place my drink coasters.

The stranger and sillier the interaction, the more likely it is to stick in your memory. In other words, don't just place a loaf of bread on top of the TV at Location 3. There's very little about that interaction between the bread and TV that makes that memorable. Instead, arrange the slices of bread as a frame around the TV or imagine the TV as the door to an oven that you open to remove the freshly baked bread.

When you're finished and standing in the grocery store, you should be able to walk through each location in your mind palace and see every item that you need to buy.

That is the process of creating a mind palace and encoding an image to each location, but how exactly can that be applied to memorizing verses in Scripture?

Biblical Application

The best way to begin using the Mind Palace method for memorizing the Bible is to start small. Put aside the urge to start memorizing an entire Pauline epistle or chapter of Romans. This method requires you to learn how to crawl before you start running.

Find a short psalm or a collection of verses like the Romans Road. It's to your benefit to be able to use the simple 11-location palace you created just a few minutes ago before you start building palaces with hundreds of locations.

The trick is to find a way to distill a verse into a single image or scene.

I'll give you an example from the mind palace I built for the book of Philippians. The palace I used was an international school that had multiple buildings as part of the complex, which meant that I could differentiate each of the four chapters based on which building I was in. Within the first building was a classroom that—at least in my mind's eye—is decorated like a casino where the only table is playing the game of Blackjack. While this may not be significant to you, my brain quickly associates the game of Blackjack with the number 21 because that's what a player needs to score to win.

Entering this room, I see that the cards I have been dealt are a four, a two, and a face card that has my face on it instead of the king. In other words, it's a me card.

Stick with me here. I know this may sound complicated, but hearing another person's mind palace always sounds complicated. It's only supposed to make sense to that person. Your palace and the images you create will make sense to you but probably sound weird to me.

This scene of a Blackjack game gives me all the information I need to remember that Philippians 1:21, which begins with "For to me, to live is Christ and to die is gain."

— Philippians is the mind palace location.

— Chapter 1 is the building in the school complex.

— Verse 21 is the classroom in the school decorated like a casino.

— "For to me" translates to the cards I've been dealt—a four and a two.

Again, everybody has their own way of creating a mind palace that works for them. Over the years that I've been tweaking this technique for myself, I've learned a few things.

* It's best to create a scene that helps me remember the first few words of a verse. Creating an image for every word in the verse tends to overload a single location.

- I frequently update my location images. During my reviews, if I find that I always forget a particular word in a verse, I add another image to that location to help me remember the word.

- I try my best to maintain a single palace for each book of the Bible that I memorize (for example, a church building or the school) and divide it out by chapter based on buildings, levels, or sections. This becomes much harder once you start to memorize longer books of the Bible, so there are advanced techniques for linking various palaces together.

- While it's not absolutely necessary, I enjoy the challenge of gluing three pieces of information together: the location, the verse number, and the image for the verse. This allows me to find verses in my mind as I study other parts of the Bible.

- I don't recommend reusing a palace location. Once I used my childhood bedroom as a mind palace for Psalm 23, I won't use it again for another passage of Scripture to avoid confusion. Don't worry about running out of palace locations. The more you practice this technique, the more you'll recognize you have an infinite number of palaces to find or create.

More Mind Palace Resources

 If all this still seems a bit confusing, don't despair! Sometimes a visual technique requires more of a visual explanation. Scan to view this playlist of videos showing my full process of creating a mind palace for Psalm 46.

MemorizeWhatMatters.com/Psalm46

But the Advocate, the Holy Spirit, whom the Father will send in my name, will teach you all things and will remind you of everything I have said to you.

John 14:26

Chapter 11
Spaced Repetition

"These techniques are great, but what's the point if I'm just going to inevitably forget them all?"

"Why should I memorize when I can't even remember it a week later?"

"If I review my verses every day, I never have time to memorize anything new."

Do any of these complaints sound familiar? We're willing to put so much time and energy into the process of memorization, but then we blame our review system, or lack thereof, when the growing mountain of memorized verses starts to crumble. Not everybody has the goal of actively retaining every Bible verse that they've memorized, but I, for one, have the desire to memorize and retain them for life.

To do this, being strategic about the review process is critical. The spaced repetition strategy transforms how I review and meditate on hard-won memorized verses.

The way brains retain and lose information has been graphed in the Forgetting Curve, an idea first developed by German psychologist Hermann Ebbinghaus in the late 1800s.

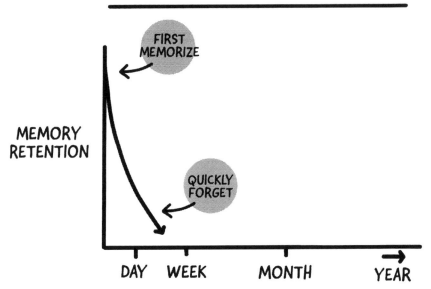

When you learn a new piece of information (a new Bible verse) or a temporary piece of information (where you put your keys), the forgetting curve is steep, which means that you're likely to forget quickly.

Evidence shows, however, that if you review the new or temporary information before it falls below a certain threshold, the forgetting curve becomes less and less steep. Eventually, the information moves to what we call our long-term memory.

Spaced repetition is a review strategy in which you review information at gradually increasing intervals.

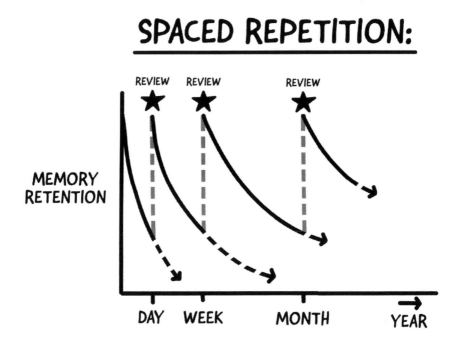

The simple guidelines of spaced repetition go like this:

- Memorize new information (a verse or passage).

- Review later that day. If you can recall the information, move to the next spaced interval; otherwise review again 12 hours later.

- Review the next day. If you can recall the information, move to the next spaced interval; otherwise move back a spaced interval.

- Review 3 days later. If you can recall the information, move to the next spaced interval; otherwise move back a spaced interval.

- Review 1 week later. If you can recall the information, move to the next spaced interval; otherwise move back a spaced interval.

- Continue increasing the spacing up to many months.

As I write this, I'm in the process of memorizing the book of 1 Peter. Since it's a new passage for me, I'm reviewing most of these verses daily until I have them down well enough to move to every 3 days and eventually to once a week.

For the book of 2 Timothy, which I memorized last year, I've spaced out my review to once every month. During that review I'll forget a word or two or maybe a verse, but the monthly review continues to move this book into long-term memory.

I memorized the book of James when I was in high school. Over the years I've reviewed this book countless times, but at this point, I've spaced out my review of James to once every three to four months, sometimes longer.

Spaced repetition is the key to long-term retention of memorized Scripture, so it's worth the time it takes to set up a good system that works for you. There are many ways to do this, some manual, some digital, so let's break these down so you can find what might work for you.

Manual Spaced Repetition Techniques

Many people enjoy creating physical index flash cards to review their memory verses. Making flash cards is only one-half of the battle, however. To leverage spaced repetition to your advantage, you need to find a way to systemize how you space out the review.

For some people, such as my friend Faith Womack, using creative means of making flash cards is also a part of the memory process. Scan to watch how she makes her cards, or visit:

MemorizeWhatMatters.com/faith

A popular way to do this is known as the Charlotte Mason Method, a philosophy of education from a British educator who lived in the late 19th century.

In this technique, index cards are placed in a box with dividers that are labeled daily, odd, even, one for every day of the week, and finally one for each of the 31 days of the month (41 total).

As you master verses, they move from the daily review section to even and odd days, followed by days of the week and the days of the month. This not only helps you space out your review, it also makes it easy to know exactly which verses you need to review for that day.

A similar but less involved method can be done with a notebook, a technique that my friend Iris showed me. Start with a notebook of lined paper and add tabs for daily, weekly, monthly, and quarterly. Write down the verses you are memorizing on the daily sheet and then check off each day you review for a set number of consecutive times (for example, 7 or 10 times to review). Once you've completed all consecutive reviews, move that verse to the weekly tab.

Scan to see me explain how Iris' manual notebook review method works, or visit:

MemorizeWhatMatters.com/notebook

Both the index cards and the notebook work well for those people who benefit from checking reviews off a list or physically seeing spaced repetition in action. Technology, however, provides some easier ways to automate the review strategy.

Digital Spaced Repetition Techniques

We have two primary ways to use digital tools to introduce spaced repetition into Bible memory review: digital flashcards and memory apps.

Digital flashcard apps such as Anki or Quizlet allow you to take your flashcards on the go, making them accessible on your mobile device or computer. The hardest part about using these apps is the time it takes to create the flashcards.

Once the flashcards have been created, the flashcard apps take all the guesswork out of review and spaced repetition. When reviewing a flashcard, you're given the option to mark it on a scale between forgotten and easily remembered, which affects how often the app brings that card back for review.

Dedicated apps such as the Bible Memory app, VerseLocker app, and the Verses app offer the same functionality with slightly differing features. With these apps, it's much easier to create flashcards because you only have to choose the verses or passages that you want to memorize and the translation you prefer. It even allows you to review your verses using the First Letter method (see

Chapter 1), where you type out the first letter of each word in a verse to demonstrate mastery.

After you've reviewed a verse on one of these Bible memory apps, spaced repetition is automatically applied to determine the next time you get tested on that verse. If you review with 100% accuracy, the spacing is increased. If you review with an accuracy below 80%, the app will likely ask you to review the verse again the next day.

Making use of these analog and digital tools for spaced repetition will not only help you review verses easily, but it will also effectively move these memorized portions of the Bible from short-term to long-term memory.

But may all who seek you, rejoice and be glad in you.

Psalm 70:4

Chapter 12
Celebrate Your Wins

Have you ever read the Old Testament and thought to yourself, *These people celebrate the tiniest of achievements?*

— Cross a river? Let's celebrate! (Exodus 15:19-21)

— Walk six steps with the ark of the covenant? Stop and celebrate! (2 Samuel 6:13)

— Have a conversation with God? Let's memorialize it! (Genesis 35:14)

Even Jesus seems to be fond of celebrating events that we don't usually consider joyous occasions, including the return of a runaway son (Luke 15).

Too often, people are afraid to celebrate for fear of appearing boastful or coming across as an arrogant super-Christian. People may think that quiet humility is the spiritual way to deal with any progress they make in their faith or pursuit of God.

While a line can certainly be crossed, I believe we err too much on the side of conservative caution. We have so much to celebrate, and the Bible gives us many examples of how God delights to see us celebrate, especially when it draws us closer to Him.

Now let's be clear about a few things before we continue: the purpose of memorizing the Bible is to know God and to build the foundation of our faith. The journey of memorizing and internalizing God's Word is where transformation happens, not at some magical moment when we've reached a certain memorization goal or finished memorizing.

That being said, we do ourselves—and even the family of God—a huge disservice when we fail to celebrate wins both big and small along the way.

Did you set a goal to memorize a verse per week for 3 months and accomplish it? *Celebrate!*

Did you memorize your first complete book, even if it was a short one? *Celebrate!*

Did you recite an entire psalm from memory? *Celebrate!*

I'll give you some examples of how you can celebrate in a moment, but first let's understand *why* it's so important to celebrate.

The Dopamine Reward

A physiological response happens in our body whenever we achieve a goal that we've set. Our brain releases dopamine, a reward chemical, which plays a critical role in our motivation to continue pursuing new goals.

The most common hurdle faced by people who memorize the Bible boils down to one thing: motivation. Maintaining a consistent habit of memorizing Scripture takes a lot of discipline, and it's very easy to get demotivated over time.

Don't worry. You're not the only one.

Harnessing the power of the dopamine reward is one way to sustain the internal drive to keep making progress while you turn Scripture memory into a daily habit. There are a few keys to succeed in setting goals that turn into habits:

- **Keep Your Goals Small.** To start, goals should be attainable in a week at most. You need to build up easy wins before you upgrade to monthly or even annual goals. Setting a long-term goal is valuable, whether you want to memorize a passage, an entire chapter, a book of the Bible or more. However, if you don't break this down into smaller goals that you can celebrate along the way, these audacious goals may prove to be discouraging. Trust me, I know.[1]

- **Track Progress.** Track the easy wins as either completed verses or a string of consecutive days that you've spent at least 5 minutes memorizing.

- **Don't Miss Twice.** There will be days when life gets in the way and perfect consistency is impossible. Give yourself grace and work hard to never miss twice.

- **Limit Who You Tell.** Research has shown that sometimes sharing your goals with others (*I'm going to memorize one verse per day this month*) can actually backfire because sharing goals gives the

---

1. I originally set a public goal of memorizing the entire New Testament in 2 years. I've had to revise my goal now that I'm on year 3 and not even halfway done.

feeling of accomplishment and satisfaction without actually doing the work. There's value in building accountability toward your goals with others, but be conservative about broadcasting goals publicly.

The Community Reward

How were you first inspired to memorize Scripture? The common story I hear over and over from people is that they heard a pastor or a friend or somebody in their church recite Scripture from memory. They thought, *Wow, that's really cool. I want to do that too.*

Because memorizing Scripture is often considered a private, personal spiritual discipline, people often fail to use it to build up the Body of Christ. Paul writes in his letter to the Ephesians: "Instead, speaking the truth in love, we will grow to become in every respect the mature body of him who is the head, that is, Christ" (Ephesians 4:15). When Paul talks about "speaking the truth in love" here, what greater truth could we speak than God's own words written in Scripture?

In a misguided effort to not look "too spiritual," people may rob brothers and sisters in Christ of an incredible encounter with God's Word that might inspire them to start their own journey of memorizing and internalizing Scripture.

People *need* to hear the Word of God spoken in our Christian communities, whether that's on a Sunday morning or in a small Bible study group.

When we talk about a community reward for reciting Scripture, it's not about a reward *you* receive for reciting what you've memorized. Rather, the reward is what the *listener* receives by hearing God's Word spoken.

How to Celebrate Your Wins

Celebrations come in many forms, so you can celebrate your big and small Scripture memory wins. Here are a few ideas to consider.

- **Celebratory Meal.** When you celebrate something, you attach importance to it. This is one way in which I share this value of Scripture memory with my family, particularly my young boys. For example, when I finish memorizing a book of the Bible, I like to take my family out to eat to celebrate.

In most cases, I've already recited the book to them, and they know the purpose of the special meal.

- **Recite to a Friend.** Invite a friend to coffee and ask if you can recite what you've memorized to them. (Be sure to pay for their coffee!) Not only are you rewarding yourself with a special outing, but you'll also encourage and inspire your friend without pressuring them in any way. Bonus points if it's a non-Christian friend who is willing to sit and listen to you recite.

- **Recite for Your Church or Small Group.** For those who are brave, consider asking your pastor or the leader of your small group if there are any opportunities to recite Scripture. Many churches would love to incorporate Scripture recitation into their service but either haven't considered it or don't know who to ask. You could open the door for others to follow.

- **Share with an Online Community.** Post a video of yourself reciting Scripture on Facebook, Instagram, TikTok, or other social media platforms. If that feels uncomfortable for you, there are places where it is entirely appropriate—even encouraged—to share your wins. In our free online Bible memory community (www.biblememorygoal.com/join), we have an entire space dedicated to sharing wins. Every day, people from all over the world post videos of themselves reciting the verses or passages that they've memorized, knowing that everybody in the community is working toward a similar goal. We encourage each other and celebrate together.

Whatever you do, remember that celebrations are not just about you. It's an opportunity to build up the body of Christ in a way that has been done throughout church history for thousands of years.

 Scan to join a community of thousands of believers around the globe who encourage each other toward Scripture memory, or visit:

BibleMemoryGoal.com/Join

Keep this Book of the Law always on your lips; meditate on it day and night, so that you may be careful to do everything written in it. Then you will be prosperous and successful.

Joshua 1:8

Epilogue

My family had begun to dread the sound of steps coming up the staircase that led to our fourth-floor apartment in China. Usually, it was our neighbors on the fifth or sixth floor, but sometimes the footsteps were followed by a knock on our door, signifying another visit from the police.

Instead of holding me in a prison cell during those days of interrogation, I had been picked up early every morning and dropped off late at night to sleep. Our passports had been taken from us along with our computers, phones, and other electronic devices. They were accusing me of being a spy and threatening me with years in prison away from my wife and two boys.

It was, without a doubt, the most difficult and challenging experience of my life to that point.

Most mornings, a knock on the door would mean another 12-hour session of questioning, but on other days, we were left completely on our own. I remember sitting on the couch on one of those days with my wife and boys, singing worship songs together as I played guitar, tears streaming down my face.

I wish I could tell you that I was a model Christian, fully trusting God and willing to accept whatever hardship He asked me to endure. I wish I could say that I rejoiced in my suffering (Romans 5:3) and considered others above my interests (Philippians 2:3–4). I wish I could tell you that every day after my interrogation session, when the police dropped me off at home telling me that this would be my last day with my family, I didn't crumple onto the floor and weep like a child.

Altogether, my family was detained and harassed for 17 days. My wife and I were both interrogated separately and accused of being spies for a foreign government. Finally, for reasons still unknown to me, the espionage accusations were abruptly dropped, and we both signed documents admitting to being Christians and sharing our faith. We were given 24 hours to leave and told we were banned from returning to China.

What I can say is that God taught me a lot during this ordeal. Proverbs 18:10 took on a whole new meaning for me. "The name of the Lord is a strong tower; the righteous man runs into it and is safe" (ESV).

The character in this short verse is under attack, and the forces of the enemy are more than he alone can handle. It feels like the spiritual thing to do is to pray, swallow his fear, and stand in godly defiance of the attack.

I don't know about you, but this is the picture I have from reading stories of persecution and martyrdom of the saints throughout history: steadfast boldness in the midst of the storm.

The verse that comes to my mind is from Joshua. "Have I not commanded you? Be strong and courageous. Do not be afraid; do not be discouraged, for the Lord your God will be with you wherever you go." (1:9)

No fear.

No doubt.

Just bravery.

For the longest time, I felt intense shame over the fact that my story didn't seem to align with this paradigm. I *was* afraid, and it *was* a daily battle for me to trust that God was in control of the situation. That's why this one proverb resonated with me so much.

The character in Proverbs 18:10, who is under attack, does not stand in holy defiance. What does he do? He turns around and runs into the strong tower. Running away, not in cowardice, but in confidence, knowing that the safety of the tower was stronger than the fear of the attack.

The best part? The Bible has a name for the person who may be filled with fear, doubt, and uncertainty about the troubles that surround them. The author of Proverbs doesn't hesitate to label the person who turns around and runs to the safety of the tower, which is the name of the Lord.

They are *righteous*.

In our journeys through life to be more like Jesus, it's very tempting to try to do it in our own strength, even if we don't realize that's what we're doing. Instead of running to the tower, we attempt to fight the battle on our own. We try to explain what we believe in our own words or pray a prayer of our own making. We build a theology based on what feels logical and develop a worldview that has less to do with what the Bible actually says and more to do with what's convenient for us. We want to be strong and courageous, just like it says in Joshua 1:9, but we tend to forget the verse that comes right before it.

"Keep this Book of the Law always on your lips; meditate on it day and night, so that you may be careful to do everything written in it. Then you will be prosperous and successful." (Joshua 1:8)

It doesn't matter what method or technique you use for memorization. The time spent internalizing God's Word is never wasted nor does it return empty (Isaiah 55:11). The effort required to sow the seeds of Scripture in our hearts and minds will "reap a harvest if we do not give up" (Galatians 6:9).

Lord willing, you'll never see the day when the Bible is banned or you find yourself locked in a prison with nothing but the clothes on your back and the scripture you can pull up from your memory.

However, regardless of future circumstances, I have yet to meet a person who regrets the time they have invested in memorizing God's Word.

My prayer for those of you who have read this book is that the Lord will stir this passion in your heart for years to come. Let's turn our focus away from all the mindless scrolling or binge watching and spend our time trying to **memorize what matters**.

 **Bible**
Memory Goal

This book is part of an ongoing effort to create the most useful and accessible Bible memory resources.

 @BibleMemoryGoal

 Memorize What Matters

 BibleMemoryGoal.com/Join

Take the next step in your Bible memory journey! Find the accountability, training and encouragement you need to internalize God's Word like never before.

MemorizeWhatMatters.com/Next-Steps

Acknowledgements

Writing a book is never a simple task, nor is it a solo one. The process of going from blank page to published book requires more than one person alone can accomplish and I'd like to take a moment to acknowledge the contributions of people who might not get named in the front matter of the book.

First, I'd like to thank my family, including my incredible wife Tiffany and my awesome boys Jaden and Josiah. Their continued support throughout this journey – not just writing a book but the journey of memorizing Scripture – is the best encouragement I can hope for.

I'm grateful for the incredible work of Vicki Newby, whose editing work went above and beyond a simple "job." I would also like to thank Debby Summers (yes, that's my mom!), Peter Allan, Peter Gee, Sheree Belfils, Debra Wyza, Ben Mitchell, Joshua Frost, Liang Wang, Garth Tanner, and Shelley Hitz who all provided great feedback on the original draft of the book, in addition to the entire team who supported the book launch.

Thanks to those of you who are part of our online Bible Memory Community. What started as a fun little project has turned into one of the most encouraging, motivating and fun places to hang out on the internet. What a privilege it is to build accountability in God's Word together!

Finally, my hope and prayer is that this book and all the work that goes into creating these Bible memory resources are counted not as any good works that I do, but rather as a sacrifice of praise to the God who has blessed me more than I deserve. To Him alone be the glory.

Made in the USA
Las Vegas, NV
28 September 2024

b8979f79-6a2b-49e8-bd6d-52d20daebd0aR02